PURSUING
IMPACT

PURSUING IMPACT

mission-driven strategic planning for nonprofits

Alicia M. Schatteman

JOHNS HOPKINS UNIVERSITY PRESS BALTIMORE

Johns Hopkins University Press
2715 North Charles Street
Baltimore, Maryland 21218
www.press.jhu.edu

Library of Congress Cataloging-in-Publication Data

Names: Schatteman, Alicia M., 1970– author.
Title: Pursuing impact : mission-driven strategic planning
for nonprofits / Alicia M. Schatteman.
Description: Baltimore : Johns Hopkins University Press, [2024] |
Includes bibliographical references and index.
Identifiers: LCCN 2023029975 | ISBN 9781421448824 (paperback) |
ISBN 9781421448831 (ebook)
Subjects: LCSH: Nonprofit organizations—Management. |
Strategic planning.
Classification: LCC HD62.6 .S34873 2024 |
DDC 346/.064—dc23/eng/20230821
LC record available at https://lccn.loc.gov/2023029975

A catalog record for this book is available from the British Library.

Special discounts are available for bulk purchases of this book.
For more information, please contact Special Sales at specialsales@jh.edu.

To the memory of my beloved mother,
HEDY A. VILLENEUVE
(1943–2022)

CONTENTS

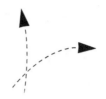

ACKNOWLEDGMENTS

THIS BOOK WOULD NOT HAVE BEEN POSSIBLE without the encouragement of my former colleague Dr. Jerry Gabris, professor emeritus in the Department of Public Administration at Northern Illinois University. He asked me to help him assist a nonprofit organization with its strategic planning process. That experience working with him sparked a joy and curiosity that still endures. Of course, I also must thank all those nonprofit organizations, over 60 to date, that have entrusted me with their challenges, their hopes, their fears, and their successes. Without those organizations, I would not have had the opportunity to think through my own process for strategic planning, which is what I share in this book.

Thanks go to my colleagues at the Center for Governmental Studies and the Department of Public Administration at Northern Illinois University and the DeKalb County Nonprofit Partnership for giving me many opportunities to present aspects of this book to their groups, which provided feedback and ideas.

Thank you to my current and former graduate and undergraduate students. I have taught courses in strategic planning over the years, and my students have always challenged my assumptions and ideas. I am eternally optimistic about the future because of them.

This book was mostly written during the pandemic, while all six of our children crowded back into the nest (Kaitlyn, Brian, Lillian, John, Sam, and Sarah). As we navigated work and school at home, my husband, Matt, gave me the space and grace to work on this book project, even converting our dining room into my home office, complete with a door (!). You are simply the best, Matt.

Finally, thank you to Laura Davulis, editor at Johns Hopkins University Press, and her team. She believed in the project from day one, and her guidance helped shape the book that is before you.

PURSUING IMPACT

INTRODUCTION

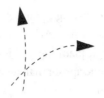

THIS BOOK IS A RESULT OF 13 years of teaching strategic planning and consulting with over 60 organizations. During this time, I was able to draw on existing literature and my professional experience in nonprofit organizations, including four years as an executive director. What I've learned over the years is that organizations often reach out to me when they need help to create a plan, a document they think will guide them magically toward a future desired state. Rarely does any document do that. Rather, I guide them through a *process*, with the view that strategic planning is similar to budgeting: it's never really "over." Especially as organizations evolve out of the pandemic, they are seeking a path forward, trying to bring some predictability and stability after having survived a tumultuous time.

When I began studying and consulting with nonprofit organizations to assist them with strategic planning, I relied heavily on frameworks developed by others and then adapted them based on an organization's needs and context. Over time, I developed the framework I share in this book. It is flexible enough to accommodate any nonprofit of any size and configuration. This book is intended to be both a practical guide and an analysis of the body of academic research on nonprofit strategic planning. In the late 1980s, John Bryson's work sought to translate the use of strategic planning from the private sector to the public sector (Bryson 1988; Bryson and Roering 1987). He then went on to research strategic planning in both the public and nonprofit sectors and perfected a methodology which has been well documented in his many articles and textbooks. Building on Bryson's work, others have tried to tease out the similarities and dissimilarities in strategic planning in all three sectors. This book is intended for academic researchers and students who are specifically interested in strategic planning in this context. It is also meant to be a practical guide for nonprofit managers and boards who want to create and guide their own strategic planning process grounded in evidence.

How Is This Book Different?

Most practical guides to strategic planning for nonprofit staff and boards are manuals or workbooks that take an organization through a series of steps to a seemingly logical conclusion. But they tend to ignore the "why" and do not acknowledge the nuances that each organization must wrestle with as it not only creates a strategic plan but implements one. This book is not just an academic treatise of the literature. Instead, it places that literature in the context of the needs of nonprofit organizations, which in this country are mainly small organizations, with budgets to match. Although the academic literature informs their management practices, I make those linkages more evident. The book is intended to be accessible to researchers and students of nonprofit management as well as to the board and staff leaders of nonprofit organizations. Topics covered in the subsequent chapters break down the strategic planning process and present it as a cycle rather than as a linear process.

Strategic planning is a core function of nonprofit organizations, specifically of nonprofit boards. One reason for developing a practitioner-centric approach to strategic planning derives from my experiences designing and facilitating strategic planning processes for nonprofit organizations. I needed a useful and flexible model to provide practical advice for nonprofit staff and boards to guide the strategic planning process. The generic model developed by Bryson (1988) downplays the numerous organizational and bureaucratic pitfalls likely to wreak havoc on the best-devised plans. Further, small non-profit organizations—which are the vast majority of nonprofits—undertake strategic planning without the guidance of a paid consultant. These boards need the most assistance to understand the process before embarking on the plan and then to guide them through it.

I have written this book to be accessible to everyone. I avoid the typical academic or impersonal passive voice and supplement the academic literature with examples from my own consulting and experiences. These examples are intended to connect the academic research to nonprofit management and governance. This book also aims to bring the academics who study strategic planning together with the practice of strategic planning. I assert that strategic planning is a cycle but that the process may not always follow the same exact steps. Sometimes organizations are in one part of the cycle but then need to go back to previous steps or start the cycle over again. For example, many organizations right now are looking at their current strategic plan, which was based on a set of assumptions that no longer apply in the post-pandemic era. They are deciding to review where they are, to revise their plans, or to begin anew.

How the Book Is Organized

In this book, I aim to bring the theory of nonprofit strategic planning together with the practice—a practical guide grounded in research. Each chapter begins with a list of key points to be discussed, then relevant research is presented, followed by practical aspects of strategic planning, and finally the chapter concludes with discussion questions. You can use these discussion questions with your students, staff, or board members to think through the concepts and keep the cycle moving forward. For a graphic of the strategic planning process and how the rest of the book is organized, see figure 1.

This book generally follows the action research model of planned change, a cyclical process (Cummings and Worley 2015). A plan is a document. This book proposes that organizations engage in a process.

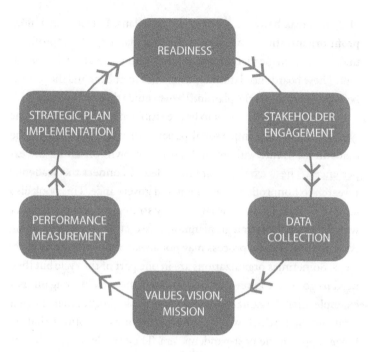

FIGURE 1
Cycle of Strategic Planning

- **CHAPTER 1** gives the background to strategic planning, definitions, and the overall approach to strategic planning as a process. Subsequent chapters address each aspect of the cyclical model.
- **CHAPTER 2** outlines how an organization goes about deciding whether it is ready to embark on or continue a strategic planning process and how to identify any barriers as well as how to reduce those barriers before proceeding to the next step.
- **CHAPTER 3** is all about stakeholder engagement. Organizations must decide who should participate through stakeholder identification as well as how to engage those stakeholders in their strategic planning process.
- **CHAPTER 4** shares techniques and methods of data collection, from administrative data to existing secondary data and primary data that need to be collected. Once collected, organizations then need to decide how to summarize and present that data to the board or the strategic planning committee so the data can inform the next step.

- **CHAPTER 5** addresses the critical role of the board in the strategic planning process with a review of the values, vision, and mission of the organization.
- **CHAPTER 6** goes into more detail about taking the critical issues the organization wants to address and moving them through a process to identify priorities and goals based on evidence.
- **CHAPTER 7** discusses resource allocation for the plan, including both the human and financial resources needed to move the plan forward. This chapter also shares how to monitor and report on the plan, creating a feedback mechanism that engages the staff and board in the plan's overall success.

REFERENCES

Bryson, J. (1988). A strategic planning process for public and non-profit organizations. *Long Range Planning* 21(1): 73–81.

Bryson, J., and Roering, W. (1987). Applying private-sector strategic planning in the public sector. *Leadership & Management* 53(1): 9–22.

Cummings, T., and Worley, C. (2015). *Organization Development and Change*. 10th ed. Mason, OH: Cengage.

CHAPTER 1

Background

"Would you tell me, please, which way I ought to go
from here?"

"That depends a good deal on where you want to get
to," said the Cat.

"I don't much care where"—said Alice.

"Then it doesn't matter which way you go," said the
Cat.

"-so long as I get somewhere," Alice added as an
explanation.

"Oh, you're sure to do that," said the Cat, "if you
only walk long enough."

(Carroll 1865)

KEY POINTS

1. The nonprofit sector in the United States provides a large scope of services with a wide variety of types of nonprofits.
2. Strategic planning is always needed—not just in times of calm but especially in times of chaos.

3. Strategic planning is a disciplined process with formal beginnings in the military.
4. Strategic planning is a cyclical process resulting in a plan that includes implementation.

Overview of the Nonprofit Sector

The nonprofit sector in the United States is large and has grown as the population has expanded, resulting in about 1.6 million registered nonprofit organizations today. Collectively, they provide vital programs and services. They range in size, from all-volunteer organizations with no revenue or staff to large entities with highly professional staff. Revenue comes from multiple sources, including individual donors, fees for service, grants, contracts, membership dues, investment and endowment income, and other earned revenue. They serve all areas of the country and every demographic.

Not only are they numerous, but nonprofit organizations also employ a significant number of people in the private workforce, 12.5 million workers, exceeding the manufacturing workforce. In terms of the overall workforce, the business sector makes up 80.5%, followed by nonprofits (6.4%), local government (6.3%), state government (4.5%), and the federal government (2.4%) (Independent Sector 2022). In education, nonprofits account for nearly three-quarters of the nation's private labor force. Other large segments of nonprofit workers are in social assistance and in health services, including hospitals and nursing homes. Nonprofits are also the third-largest generator of payroll income after professional and technical services and manufacturing. Nonprofits increased their workforce by 18% over the period 2007 to 2017, compared to 6% growth in the for-profit sector (Salamon and Newhouse 2020).

Nonprofit organizations are regulated by the Internal Revenue Service (IRS), which grants organizations nonprofit status under the tax code. Organizations are classified as one of several nonprofit categories. The most common type, 501(c)(3), is unique among the categories. This type of nonprofit must provide broad public benefit to society, which then allows it to receive tax-deductible donations. The 501(c)(3) organizations account for about three-quarters of all registered nonprofits (NCCS 2021). In addition to the IRS, nonprofits are regulated by each state's attorney general's office. State attorneys general are charged with protecting consumers and ensuring that nonprofit organizations comply with legal requirements in that state.

To understand the scope of the sector, a consistent classification system was developed in the 1980s called the National Taxonomy of Exempt Entities (NTEE) system, now used by the IRS and the National Center for Charitable Statistics. The NTEE classification system divides the universe of nonprofit organizations into 26 major groups under 10 broad categories: Arts, Culture, and Humanities (A); Education (B); Environment and Animals (C, D); Health (E, F, G, H); Human Services (I, J, K, L, M, N, O, P); International, Foreign Affairs (Q); Public, Societal Benefit (R, S, T, U, V, W); Religion Related (X); Mutual/Membership Benefit (Y); Unknown and Unclassified (Z). Within the major groups, organizations are further broken down according to logical divisions and subdivisions (Jones 2019). The National Center for Charitable Statistics has also developed a complementary taxonomy in the Nonprofit Program Classification (NPC) system. Created in the early 2000s, this classification system differs from the NTEE in its focus on the activities and programs of the nonprofit organization rather than the type of organization (Lampkin, Romeo, and Finnin 2001).

To improve financial transparency of organizations, an organization called Philanthropic Research Inc. launched to provide data and information on America's charities. This organization became a nonprofit in 1996 and was renamed GuideStar (https://www .guidestar.org). It began reporting on 40,000 public charities, including basic financial information, which they shared on their website. In 1998, they added each charity's IRS 990 form (the tax return prepared by organizations exempt from income tax). By 2001, their database included all 501(c)(3) organizations, and it was expanded again in 2005 to include all nonprofit organizations. GuideStar offers free access to PDF versions of the IRS 990 forms and basic financial information. Premium access (paid membership) allows individuals to search, save, and download financial information. You can search the database with key attributes of geography (state, zip code, metro statistical area, city, county), organization (GuideStar Seal of Transparency, subject area, populations served, affiliation type, number of employees, diversity, IRS form type and audits), and financials (revenue, total expenses, total assets).

History of Strategic Planning

Strategic planning in nonprofit organizations follows in the footsteps of planning in the private and public sectors. Public administration scholars have examined the importance of goal setting for some time. Luther Gulick, an early public management scholar, coined the acronym POSDCORB to describe the various tasks of public management: planning, organizing, staffing, directing, coordinating, reporting, and budgeting. Planning, mentioned first, referred to the critical function of planning for the future (Gulick 1937). Another classic public administration scholar was Herbert Simon. Simon received both his BA (1936) and his PhD (1943) in political science from the University of Chicago, and he had also been a research assistant for Clarence Ridley. At the time, Ridley was the executive director of the International City Managers' Association (ICMA). Later, Simon became a professor of political science at the Illinois Institute of Technology and spent most of his career at Carnegie Mellon University (1949–2001). Today we would call Simon an interdisciplinary scholar, studying and conducting research in economics, political science, public administration, management, psychology, and computer science. He even received the Nobel Prize in Economics in 1978. He is best known for his theories of bounded rationality and satisficing (Simon 1945). Simon believed managers needed to "satisfice" when decision-makers could not determine an optimal solution, much like operating during a pandemic. Given that decision-makers in the practical world do not always have all the needed information, managers must still make a decision, or "satisfice" (1945).

In practice, strategic planning has its roots in the military, where it was used to organize resources to be comprehensively prepared for any potential scenario (Sutherland 1978). The private sector embraced strategic planning in the middle of the twentieth century (Moskow 1978). Government agencies have used strategic planning since at least the late 1980s, which is in line with new public management and adoption of business practices in the public sector (Osborne and Gaebler 1992; Bryson 1988; Denhardt 1983). Berry's research on the adoption of strategic planning by state agencies in 1999 noted four factors that lead to adoption: resources, leadership cycle, orientation to business and citizens, and diffusion of strategic planning across states (Berry 1999). These factors can also inform a strategic planning process in the nonprofit sector to some degree, although the context does matter.

Strategic planning attempts to predict an unknown and changing future, which contrasts with long-range planning, where resources are organized in the context of a known future in which the environment is static and predictable (Kaye 2005; Bryson 1999). By the 1990s, other units of government began using strategic planning to facilitate organizational change and better meet community needs (Denhardt and Denhardt 2015; Berry 1994; Osborne and Gaebler 1992). Initiatives were often adopted by state agency leaders who were influenced by neighboring organizations that used strategic planning tactics or by the hiring of new managers familiar with strategic planning practices (Berry 1994). Strategic planning spread in spite of many believing it "corporatized" the public sector (Stone 1989). Scholarship exploring strategic plan formulation flourished, as well as "how-to" manuals designed for practitioners (Andrews et al. 2012; Bryson 2011; Rowman, Littlefield, and La Pianna 2008; Sagini 2007; Allison and Kaye 2005; Bryson 1999).

A second factor encouraging more rigorous strategic planning practices was the growing literature on public sector planning methodology. Bryson's model was a major advancement for explaining not only *why* public and nonprofit organizations should have a strategic plan but *how* to plan (Bryson 2011). Until his work, there were no clear or accessible models. Other scholars began contributing to this nascent literature, however, offering advice not only to managers but, just as importantly, to consultants who often provided technical expertise for formulating better strategic plans (Bryson 2011; Burkhart and Reuss 1993).

A third factor influencing government agencies to take strategic planning more seriously involved the growing body of research advocating for greater citizen involvement and democratic accountability (Denhardt and Denhardt 2015; Kelman and Myers 2011). Strategic planning presented an excellent opportunity for the public to influence an organization's future by accessing the planning process and offering their ideas. Ultimately, new public service developed from public participation and enhanced democratic values (Denhardt and Denhardt 2015).

At the same time, both political and academic stakeholders questioned the competency and capacity of government organizations to efficiently carry out their missions (Gore 1996; Osborne and Gaebler 1992). Government organizations were perceived as highly inefficient, stagnant, and inept monopolies resistant to change. Administrators and elected officials began to realize the expectations and assumptions historically providing them unquestioned support had dissipated. Stakeholders expected public and nonprofit organizations to be entrepreneurial, adaptive, market competitive, results driven, customer oriented, and capable of thinking strategically (Donald, Lyons, and Tribbey 2001; Siciliano 1997; Wesley, Stone, and Crittenden 1994; Osborne and Gaebler 1992). Not surprisingly, the new forces shaping these organizations emanated from the private sector. If an organization could not efficiently respond to heightened demands for service, then perhaps its function should be privatized. Government agencies received the message, and a new era dawned in which the public sector embraced decision-making techniques, like strategic planning, originally developed in the private sector to help it flourish and prosper; this new age is often referred to as the era of new public management (Kearney and Coggburn 2016; Bowman 2008; Poister and Streib 2005). Prior to the 2000s, numerous local governments involved the governing board and the most senior staff person only. Today most organizations benefit from more mature and productive relationships with administrative staff and consider them a trusted governance partner (Gabris and Nelson 2013).

Like the public sector, the nonprofit sector also adopted businesslike practices as part of the new public management era. Furthermore, collaboration between the three sectors continued to grow through the 1990s and early 2000s, as several researchers have noted (Austin 2000; Alexander and Weiner 1998; Gilmour and Jensen 1998; Smith and Lipsky 1993). Competition increased for philanthropic dollars, at the same time as responsibility for public services shifted from government to private and nonprofit sectors (Alexander and Weiner 1998). Salamon (2002) referred to this phenomenon as "new governance," where lines blurred between the sectors. "A host of non-governmental, third-party surrogates or proxies . . . provide programs under the aegis of loans, loan guarantees, grants, contracts, vouchers and other new tools of public action" (Hall and Kennedy 2008, 307). In 2007, this corporatization of the nonprofit sector was noted by the Panel on the Nonprofit Sector and the American Law Institute. Their subsequent report was the subject of an essay by Sugin (2007) on the "corporatization of nonprofit governance." She reiterated the unique fiduciary responsibilities of nonprofit board members to adhere to a duty of loyalty, a duty of care, and a duty of obedience. Donors are not investors or owners, unlike participants in the private sector. Donations are not contracts between nonprofits and donors, like a business transaction. Instead, donations can and should support the broader charitable use because the public interest is broader than the simple donor transaction.

More specifically related to strategic planning, Hall and Kennedy (2008) researched community-based organizations across the United States to determine the variables associated with an effective and accountable nonprofit organization. Strategic planning was strongly related to program effectiveness (Hall and Kennedy 2008). Alexander and Weiner (1998) suggested that the traditional philanthropic model of governance had shifted to a corporate model of nonprofit governance, with more emphasis on strategic activity rather than mission preservation; however, their study consisted only of nonprofit community hospitals. Although informative, more research into nonprofit organizations was needed to truly understand whether strategic planning was being used by nonprofits, under what conditions, and whether adoption and implementation drove performance. Bryson, a leading scholar in this area, wrote the major textbooks on the subject (Bryson and Slyke 2018; Bryson 2015; Bryson 2011; Bryson and Alston 2011; Bryson, Anderson, and Alston 2011; Bryson 1988; Bryson and Roering 1987). He noted that the five general steps in strategic planning may be the same in the private sector, but they cannot be exactly replicated by nonprofit organizations because of the expanded number of stakeholders, conflicting definitions of performance, public accountability, and the nature of nonprofit services. By the 1990s, potential funders often required nonprofits to have a strategic plan to qualify for grants; this meant critical financial issues facilitated the creation of a plan (Webster and Wylie 1988; Feinstein 1985; DiMaggio and Powell 1983). Because funders did not require the actual implementation of the plan, however, new forces reframed how nonprofit organizations understood and practiced strategic planning.

In 1994, Stone and Crittendon noted gaps in our understanding of strategic planning in nonprofit organizations, notably strategy formulation, strategy content, strategy implementation, performance, and governance. Nonprofit organizations use different strategic planning tools and measures of performance. Furthermore, they operate within a larger community ecosystem and therefore have many more stakeholders engaged in their work. Pressure from an external source such as a parent organization or funder can influence the adoption of strategic planning. Board governance likely influences adoption of a strategic plan, and some research supports that hypothesis (Siciliano 1997; Jenster and Overstreet 1990; Unterman and Davis 1982). In 2000, researchers examined organizational characteristics and strategic planning processes in nonprofit organizations (Crittendon and Crittendon 2000). They found that about 46% of the respondents indicated their organization had a formal written strategic plan, compared to 80–94% of for-profit companies (2000). Most nonprofits had four-to-six-year plans. Nonprofits were more likely to engage external stakeholders if they were externally oriented and had paid staff. Other research shows nonprofits were also more likely to engage in strategic planning if they had larger staff, were older, and had larger budgets (Dart et al. 1996; Wolch and Rocha 1993; Stone 1989; Webster and Wylie 1988).

Strategic planning is also related to the organization's commitment to accountability. Specifically, researchers determined that staff competency, technological resources, learning climate, and strategic planning positively demonstrated upward, lateral, and downward accountability (Bryan, Robichau, and L'Esperance 2020). See chapter 6 for more about the use of performance information in the strategic planning process.

Today nonprofit organizations are increasing their use of strategic planning, which can actually be fun for staff and volunteers. While the plan-formulation stage can be inspiring to stakeholders, buy-in can wane precipitously in the face of ongoing implementation and difficult organizational change, however. As Bryson aptly remarks, strategic planning can be defined as the enforcement of a formal discipline on a nonprofit organization by committing it to fundamental long-term goals that a typically short-term orientation does not allow (Bryson 2011). Strategic planning provides organizations a mechanism for fostering a higher level of efficiency and rationality, as long as the organization remains disciplined. Implementation requires dedication while simultaneously attending to the daily operations of the organization—planning ahead while keeping the lights on. Furthermore, bureaucratically structured organizations are subject to dysfunction and are often unfriendly toward creativity and ingenuity. Scholarship developed in the laboratories of public service organizations offers a rich understanding of real issues facing administrators (Perry 2015). Unfortunately the knowledge gap between practitioners and academics is wide (Battaglio and Scicchitano 2013)

Strategic planning initiatives are frequently used as an integral component of an organization's budgetary process, where strategic action plans further determine the high-priority goals and objectives of operating departments beyond normal fiscal years. See chapter 7 for more about implementation, including budgeting. Strategic planning for nonprofit organizations, while relying on techniques common to both the public and private sectors, is substantively different in how it is conducted and how its outcomes are used. In nonprofit organizations specifically, key stakeholders include a volunteer board of directors, members, funding bodies such as foundations or government, and beneficiaries of their services.

In more recent years, as networks and collaboration grow between and across sectors, there is a new process emerging, called Strategic Doing (https://strategicdoing.net). The creators of Strategic Doing argue that their process is particularly well suited for open and loosely connected networks (Morrison et al. 2019). I would argue that Strategic Doing does not replace strategic planning for most organizations; but for those organizations embedded in larger and more connected networks, Strategic Doing is another option. I hope that this book demonstrates the flexibility of strategic planning that works, especially for small and medium-sized organizations. It does not have to be a long and tedious process, as many might have experienced. It can be done efficiently and effectively. It does, however, require a concerted effort and a willingness to be open to possibility and change. Why do certain organizations voluntarily embrace strategic planning? Some of that may be explained by organizational culture.

Organizational Culture

Organizational culture studies looked at characteristics of organizational culture as static elements instead of how culture influences organizational functions. Beginning in the 1970s with a call for reform of the public sector, the introduction of the new public management model, and the reinventing movement offered by Osborne and Gaebler, public agencies have undertaken many initiatives to change the culture of government (1992). The notion is that government is moving away from a rational culture to a more developmental culture, emphasizing cooperation, teamwork, and entrepreneurialism.

In the 1980s the term "organizational culture" was relatively new, according to Pacanowsky and O'Donnell-Trujillo (1983). Most research to date had been "conceptual in nature," without any empirical evidence. Many ideas were speculated and theorized, but little was known with any degree of certainty. Sotirin worked to define "organizational culture" as "the amalgam of beliefs, mythology, values, and rituals that, even more than [the organization's] products, differentiates it from other organizations" (Sotirin 1984, 1). In her paper, she described the theory and research directions of organizational communication and culture at that time. The notion of how communication influences culture dates back to that time. It would be several more years before we examined how culture influences communication.

Glaser, Zamanou, and Hacker admitted that researchers needed to move beyond a normative definition of organizational culture and that the concept instead needed to be operationalized and measured (1987, 191). They developed the Organizational Culture Survey with 62 questions that were administered to a total of 138 employees of a private manufacturing company and 195 employees of a governmental agency (Glaser 1983). The study represented "a replicable effort to access organizational culture both quantitatively and qualitatively" (Glaser, Zamanou, and Hacker 1987, 191).

Zammuto and Krakower (1991) studied organizational culture in 332 colleges and universities with a survey based on the "competing values" model. They contrasted the quantitative results of the survey with a qualitative investigation of two institutions in the sample. The competing values model had been suggested earlier by Quinn and Rohrbaugh (1983; 1981). Later, Quinn and Kimberly (1984) used the model to examine organizational culture. The competing values model suggested that there are four ideal types of organizational cultures: group culture, developmental culture, hierarchical culture, and rational culture. Each type of culture has value dimensions, organizational characteristics, organizational form, and strategic orientation (table 1).

The four types of organizational cultures are ideals. An organization is unlikely to be just one type; rather, it is more likely to be

TABLE 1. THE COMPETING VALUES MODEL

	Group culture	Developmental culture	Hierarchical culture	Rational culture
Value dimensions				
People vs. organization	People	Organization	People	Organization
Flexibility vs. control	Flexibility	Flexibility	Control	Control
Means	Cohesion, morale	Adaptability, readiness	Information management, communication	Planning, goal setting
Ends	Development of human resources	Growth, resource acquisition	Stability, control	Production, efficiency
Organizational characteristics				
Compliance	Affiliation	Ideology	Rules	Contract
Motivation	Attachment	Growth	Security	Competence
Leadership	Concerned, supportive	Inventive, risk taking	Conservative, cautious	Directive, goal oriented
Organizational form	Clan	Adhocracy	Hierarchy	Market
Strategic orientation	Implementer	Stage II organization	Defender	Prospector

Source: Adapted from Quinn and Kimberly 1984

multicultural, changing depending on a particular task, activity, or goal. In Zammuto and Krakower's study of institutions of higher education, they created a survey with a series of statements, and managers could determine how they felt about a particular statement. Their responses would be indicative of that particular organization's culture or cultures. This was one of the early attempts to operationalize the competing values model of organizational culture. The results gave an overall score for each of the four culture types by individual and then an average for each institution studied.

The correlations indicated that cultural type is related to differences in organizational culture, which became a launchpad for further study of other types of organizations. Their study proved it was possible to quantifiably study organizational culture. Also, it showed that generally, organizations have multiple cultures represented, although some may be more dominant than others. Different kinds of organizations are likely to have different cultural maps, or culture profiles. The statements used by Zammuto and Krakower continue to be used by organizational culture researchers, including this study. How they mapped their results is shown in figure 2.

The competing values framework (1991) has been used in many subsequent studies. More recently, Parker and Bradley (2000) examined organizational culture in the public sector of Queensland, Australia, focusing on six organizations. They wanted to determine

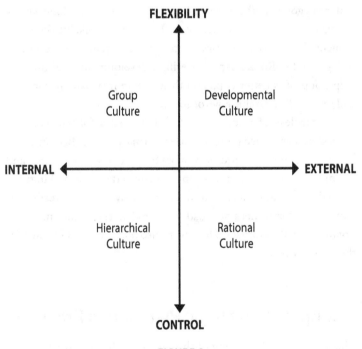

FIGURE 2
Competing Values Map
Adapted from Zammuto and Krakower 1991

whether the public sector adopted a culture of change, flexibility, entrepreneurialism, outcomes, efficiency, and productivity. They found that these six public-sector organizations continue to express the cultural values associated with bureaucratic and hierarchical organizational cultures. The traditional bureaucratic model and rational culture are still the dominant cultures, "involving hierarchical culture, regardless of policy prescriptions designed to achieve organizational change" (2000). Even though the more flexible organizational culture is desired in the private sector, perhaps it doesn't fit the public or nonprofit sectors because of the different values and motives of their employees. Organizational culture can be a process by which organizations change and react (Pacanowsky and O'Donnell-Trujillo 1983; 1982). Researchers have also used the Competing Values Culture Framework to examine how culture affects nonprofit organizational effectiveness. A developmental organizational culture that is categorized as being strong in innovation and risk taking is likely to help nonprofits achieve their goals. They are more likely to be entrepreneurial, and to seek ways to grow and acquire new resources (Langer and LeRoux 2017). Fostering a developmental culture may help nonprofits better cope and thrive in an increasingly complex and financially unstable environment.

Regardless of size, nonprofits that used a formal planning process outperformed those with a less formal practice (Bryson 2015). The benefits included promotion of strategic thinking, acting, and learning across the organization; improved decision-making; enhanced organizational effectiveness, responsiveness, and resilience; enhanced effectiveness of broader societal systems; and improved organizational legitimacy. There were also positive direct benefits for the people involved.

Nonprofit Strategic Planning in Practice

The quote at the beginning of this chapter is from Lewis Carroll's *Alice's Adventures in Wonderland*, published in 1865. The sentiment— that you need to plan a clear path forward, or you will wander aimlessly—has been repeated in other books and songs over the years. Antoine de Saint-Exupéry was a French writer, aviator, and philosopher. He wrote about the importance of goal setting in his children's novel *The Little Prince*, published in 1943: "a goal without a plan is just a wish." Later, George Harrison wrote the song "Any Road" in 1988, and he used this phrase: "and if you don't know where you're going, any road will take you there." These references suggest that a life without planning may lead to accidental success, but it may not be the best way to reach your goals.

Nonprofit organizations are under incredible financial stress as they deal with the multitude of issues brought on by the pandemic. Some may not make it. Some will close temporarily and then resurface. Some have never stopped operating and are even seeing increases in their request for service delivery, such as food and employment assistance. Although difficult to think beyond immediate needs, some nonprofit organizations use strategic planning as a key component of their decision-making processes. Others do not. Strategic planning is a demonstration of organizational leadership.

What does it mean to think strategically about an organization's future? It generally means being thoughtful and critical of every opportunity or setback that occurs inside and outside a nonprofit organization. Strategic planning should reduce your overall anxiety and improve productivity, not the other way around. This book will review the stages of a nonprofit and why the stages matter to strategic planning. For now, think about an organization you know that is just beginning: a bright and shiny nonprofit with all the board members keen and excited about this new passion and purpose. They are just spinning, dreaming about all they want to do to improve the world. They are high energy and extremely committed to a mission. Those bright eyes, however, will dim—not necessarily with wisdom, but sometimes with sheer exhaustion from trying to do it all, trying to run in all directions without a clear focus. That early passion starts to bump into the hard realities of time, of commitments outside of this nonprofit organization such as careers and family life; all these things can be put aside for a time, but they eventually start to clamor for attention. This is a critical moment for a nonprofit. Should the founders keep going? Is this personal sacrifice working for their careers, which may be funding the nonprofit, or for their families, who may be missing them on vacations or weekends? No one can answer those questions for founding board members. Likely, some of the original members will depart the organization to focus on other things. New board members will join, and the organization will begin to move into the second stage of its life, or it may have lived out its purpose and cannot sustain itself. Nonprofit organizations, just like new businesses, do fail, but nonprofit founders are tenacious and passionate. To read more about nonprofit organizational lifecycles, I recommend *Building Nonprofit Capacity* (Brothers and Sherman 2012).

➤ case example #1

An organization was founded 15 years ago by a small group of very passionate community-minded individuals who really wanted to meet residents' food needs, which were growing. Because of funding constraints, the organization was operated completely by volunteers, but they were wearing out, trying to do it all. They felt they needed someone who could take on some administrative responsibilities for the organization so some volunteers could take a step back. But there were still decisions to be made, and they knew they needed a strategic planning process to help them evaluate where they wanted to go, because not everyone was in agreement right now. After working through the process, they determined that a contract staff person could take on most of what they needed for the next two years, and then they would reevaluate for the next strategic planning process. They would be intentional about monitoring their progress to see whether they needed to adjust the timeline or the responsibilities of their contract support person.

⋀

The significant financial shock of the 2008 recession certainly affected nonprofit organizations, although differently than the pandemic. *Nonprofit Quarterly* published numerous articles comparing the last recession to what happened during the pandemic (McCambridge and Dietz 2020). The resilience of nonprofit organizations certainly proved itself during the recession. Most organizations fared well, although organizations that were weak before the recession certainly did not do as well. We are seeing the same thing today. Nonprofits that are guided by strong boards, adhere to the best practices of financial management, and communicate to their donors and staff effectively all have a fighting chance at success on the other side of the pandemic. Others do not. To what extent their behaviors and choices are the result of solid strategic planning is unknown, but those that are planning for the future are likely able to see a clear path forward.

The pandemic brought considerable changes for nonprofit organizations, including changes to revenue from contributions, changes to program services, a rise in costs for COVID-19 protections for staff and those they serve, a decreased fundraising ability, reduced volunteer support, a competitive labor market, and more. All these changes tested nonprofits' ability to adapt. Furthermore, the pandemic sped up the necessity for decisions, often with little or no information on the short-term or long-term implications of those decisions. Few organizations could have even tried to prepare for the pandemic of 2020. COVID-19 disrupted the usual board-governance models, and the best boards will adjust and anticipate the next disruption (McMullin and Raggo 2020). Strategic planning does take leadership and a commitment to managing the changes required.

DISCUSSION QUESTIONS

1. What differences and similarities are there in strategic planning in for-profit, government, and nonprofit organizations?
2. How can strategic planning be implemented in small nonprofit organizations without any paid staff?
3. Why is strategic planning a core function of a nonprofit board?
4. How can an organization's culture affect the strategic planning process?

REFERENCES

Alexander, J., and Weiner, B. (1998). The adoption of the corporate governance model by nonprofit organizations. *Nonprofit Management and Leadership* 8(3): 223–242.

Allison, M., and Kaye, J. (2005). *Strategic Planning for Nonprofit Organizations.* San Francisco: Wiley & Sons.

Andrews, R., Boyne, G., Law, J., and Walker, R. (2012). *Strategic Management and Public Service Performance.* New York: Springer.

Austin, J. E. (2000). Strategic collaboration between nonprofits and businesses. *Nonprofit and Voluntary Sector Quarterly* 29: 69–97.

Banks, S. P. (1995). *Multicultural Public Relations: A Social-Interpretive Approach.* Newbury Park, CA: Sage.

Barnard, C. (1938). *The Functions of the Executive.* Cambridge, MA: Harvard University Press.

Battaglio, R. P., and Scicchitano, M. J. (2013). Building bridges? An assessment of academic and practitioner perceptions with observations for the public administration classroom. *Journal of Public Affairs Education* 19: 749–772.

Berry, F. S. (1994). Innovation in public management: The adoption of strategic planning. *Public Administration Review* 54: 322–330.

Berry, F. S. (1999). Innovation in public management: The adoption of strategic planning. *Public Administration Review* 54(4): 322–330.

Brothers, J., and Sherman, A. (2012). *Building Nonprofit Capacity: A Guide to Managing Change Through Organizational Lifecycles.* San Francisco: Wiley & Sons.

Bowman, J. S. (2008). Turbulence in the civil service: Whither the public service ethos? In *Public Human Resource Management: Problems and Prospects,* 5th ed., edited by Steven W. Hays, Richard C. Kearney, and Jerrell D. Coggburn, 327–338. Englewood Cliffs: Prentice-Hall.

Bryan, T., Robichau, R., and L'Esperance, G. (2020). Conducting and utilizing evaluation for multiple accountabilities: A study of nonprofit evaluation capacities. *Nonprofit Management and Leadership* 31(3): 403–624. https://doi.org/10.1002/nml.21437.

Bryson, J. (1988). A strategic planning process for public and non-profit organizations. *Long Range Planning* 21(1): 73–81.

Bryson, J. (1999). *Strategic Management in Public and Voluntary Services: A Reader.* New York: Pergamon.

Bryson, J. (2011). *Strategic Planning for Public and Nonprofit Organizations.* San Francisco: Jossey-Bass.

Bryson, J. (2015). Strategic planning for public and nonprofit organizations. *International Encyclopedia of the Social and Behavioral Sciences* 2nd ed. 515–521.

Bryson, J. (2015). The future of public and nonprofit strategic planning in the United States. Supplement, *Public Administration Review* 70: S255–S267.

Bryson, J., and Alston, F. (2011). *Creating Your Strategic Plan.* San Francisco: Jossey-Bass.

Bryson, J., Anderson, S., and Alston, F. (2011). *Implementing and Sustaining Your Strategic Plan: A Workbook for Public and Nonprofit Organizations.* San Francisco: Jossey-Bass.

Bryson, J., Edwards, L., and Van Slyke, D. (2018). Getting strategic about strategic planning research. *Public Management Review* 20(3): 317–339.

Bryson, J., and Roering, W. (1987). Applying private-sector strategic planning in the public sector. *Journal of the American Planning Association* 53(1): 9–22.

Bryson, J. M. (2011). *Strategic Planning for Public and Nonprofit Organizations: A Guide to Strengthening and Sustaining Organizational Achievement.* 4th ed. Hoboken: Wiley.

Burkhart, P. J., and Reuss, S. (1993). *Successful Strategic Planning: A Guide for Nonprofit Agencies and Organizations.* Newbury Park: Sage.

Carroll, L. (1865). *Alice's Adventures in Wonderland.* London: Macmillan.

Crittendon, W. and Crittendon, V. (2000). Relationships between organizational characteristics and strategic planning processes in nonprofit organizations. *Journal of Managerial Issues* 12(2): 150–168.

Cummings, T., and Worley, C. (2015). *Organization Development and Change.* 10th ed. Stamford, CT: Cengage Learning.

Dart, R., Bradshaw, P., Murray, V., and Wolpin, J. (1996). Boards of directors in nonprofit organizations: Do they follow a life cycle model?. *Nonprofit Management and Leadership* 6(4): 367–379.

De Saint-Exupéry, A. (1943). *The Little Prince.* New York: Reynal & Hitchcock.

Denhardt, R. B., and Denhardt, J. V. (2015). *The New Public Service: Serving Not Steering.* 4th ed. New York: Routledge.

DiMaggio, P., and Powell, W. W. (1983) The iron cage revisited: Collective rationality and institutional isomorphism in organizational fields. *American Sociological Review* 48(2): 147–160.

Donald, C. G., Lyons T. S., and Tribbey, R. (2001). A partnership for strategic planning and management in a public organization. *Public Performance and Management Review* 25: 176–193.

Feinstein, K. W. (1985) Innovative management in turbulent times: Large-scale agency change. *Administration in Social Work* 9, no. 3 (Fall 1985): 35–46.

Gabris, G. T, and Nelson, K. (2013). Transforming municipal boards into accountable, high performing teams: Toward a diagnostic model of governing board effectiveness. *Public Performance and Management Review* 36: 472–495.

Geertz, C. (1973). *The Interpretation of Cultures.* New York: Basic Books.

Gilmour, R. S., and Jensen, L. S. 1998. Reinventing government accountability: Public functions, privatization, and the meaning of "state action." *Public Administration Review* 58: 247–258.

Glaser, S. (1983). Assessing organizational culture: An interpretive approach. A paper presented at the Speech Communication Association Convention, Washington, DC.

Glaser, S., Zamanou, S., and Hacker, K. (1987). Measuring and interpreting organizational culture. *Management Communication Quarterly* 1(2): 173–198.

Gore, A. (1996). *The Best Kept Secrets in Government: How the Clinton Administration Is Reinventing the Way Washington Works.* Washington, DC: Government Printing Office.

Gulick, L. (1937). Notes on the theory of organization. In *Papers on the Science of Administration*, 3–13. New York: Institute of Public Administration.

Hall, L. M., and Kennedy, S. S. (2008). Public and nonprofit management and the "new governance." *American Review of Public Administration* 38(3): 307–321.

Independent Sector. (2022). *Health of the U.S. Nonprofit Sector: A Quarterly Review.* Washington, DC: Independent Sector. https://independentsector.org/resource/health-of-the-u-s-nonprofit-sector/.

Jenster, P. V., and Overstreet, J. (1990). Planning for a not-profit service: A study of US credit unions. *Long Range Planning* 23(2): 103–111.

Kearney, R., and Coggburn, J. (2016). *Public Human Resource Management.* 6th ed. Los Angeles: CQ Press.

Kelman, S., and Myers, J. (2011). Successfully achieving ambitious goals in government: An empirical analysis. *American Review of Public Administration* 41: 235–262.

La Piana, D. (2008). *The Nonprofit Strategy Revolution: Real-Time Strategic Planning in a Rapid-Response World.* St. Paul, MN: Fieldstone Alliance, Inc.

Langer, J., and LeRoux, K. (2017). Developmental culture and effectiveness in nonprofit organizations. *Public Performance and Management Review* 40(3): 457–479.

Levine, C. (1978). Organizational decline and cutback management. *Public Administration Review* 38(2): 316–325.

MacManus, T. (2000). Public relations: The cultural dimension. In *Perspectives on Public Relations Research*, edited by D. Moss, D. Vercic, and G. Warnaby, 159–178. London: Routledge.

McCambridge, R., and Dietz, N. (2020). Nonprofits in recession: Winners and losers. *Nonprofit Quarterly*, March 19, 2020.

McMullin, C., and Raggo, P. (2020). Leadership and governance in times of crisis: A balancing act for nonprofit boards. *Nonprofit and Voluntary Sector Quarterly* 49(6): 1182–1190.

Morrison, E., Hutcheson, S., Nilsen, E., Fadden, J., and Franklin, N. (2019). *Strategic Doing: Ten Skills for Agile Leadership*. Hoboken, NJ: Wiley & Sons.

Moskow, M. H. (1978). *Strategic Planning in Business and Government*. New York: Committee for Economic Development.

Jones, D. (2019). NTEE Core Codes (NTEE-CC) Overview. Washington, DC: National Center for Charitable Statistics. https://nccs.urban.org /project/national-taxonomy-exempt-entities-ntee-codes.

National Center for Charitable Statistics. (2021). *Nonprofit Trends and Impacts 2021*. Washington, DC: National Center for Charitable Statistics. https://www.urban.org/sites/default/files/publication/104889 /nonprofit-trends-and-impacts-2021_2.pdf.

Osborne, D., and Gaebler, T. (1992). *Reinventing Government*. Boston: Addison-Wesley.

Pacanowsky, M., and O'Donnell-Trujillo, N. (1982). Communication and organizational cultures. *Western Journal of Speech Communications* 46 (Spring 1982): 115–130.

Pacanowsky, M., and O'Donnell-Trujillo, N. (1983). Organizational communication as cultural performance. *Communication Monographs* 50: 126–147.

Pandey, S. K., and Garnett, J. (2006). Exploring public sector communication performance: Testing a model and drawing implications. *Public Administration Review* 66(1): 37–51.

Pandey, S. K., and Moynihan, D. P. (2005). Bureaucratic red tape and organizational performance: Testing the moderating role of culture and political support. La Follette School Working Paper No. 2005–026. http://ssrn.com/abstract=867124.

Parker, R., and Bradley, L. (2000). Organisational culture in the public sector: Evidence from six organisations. *International Journal of Public Sector Management* 13(2): 125–141.

Perry, J. L. (2015). Forging practitioner-scholar partnerships. *Public Administration Review* 75: 343–344.

Poister, T. H., and Streib, G. (2005). Elements of strategic planning and management in municipal government: Status after two decades. *Public Administration Review* 65: 45–56.

Quinn, R., and Rohrbaugh, J. (1981). A competing values approach to organizational effectiveness. *Public Productivity Review* 2: 122–140.

Quinn, R., and Rohrbaugh, J. (1983). A spatial model of effectiveness criteria: Toward a competing value approach to organizational analysis. *Management Science* 29(3): 363–377.

Quinn, R. E., and Hall, R. H. (1983). Environments, organizations and policymakers: Toward and integrative framework. In *Organizational Theory and Public Policy*, edited by R. H. Hall and R. E. Quinn, 281–298. Beverly Hills: Sage.

Quinn, R. E., and Kimberly, J. R. (1984). Paradox, planning and perseverance: Guidelines for managerial practice. In *Managing Organizational Translations*, edited by J. R. Kimberly and R. E. Quinn, 295–313. Beverly Hills: Sage.

Rubin, I. (1990). Managing cycles of growth and decline. In *Handbook of Public Administration*, edited by James L. Perry, 559–572. San Francisco: Jossey-Bass.

Sagini, M. (2007). *Strategic Planning and Management in Public Organizations.* Lanham, MD: Rowman and Littlefield.

Salamon, L. M., ed. (2002). *The Tools of Government: A Guide to the New Governance.* New York: Oxford University Press.

Salamon, L. M., and Newhouse, C. (2020). The 2020 nonprofit employment report. *Nonprofit Economic Bulletin no. 48.* Baltimore: Johns Hopkins Center for Civil Society Studies. http://ccss.jhu.edu/wp-content /uploads/downloads/2020/06/2020-Nonprofit-Employment-Report _FINAL_6.2020.pdf.

Siciliano, J. I. (1997). The relationship between formal planning and performance in nonprofit organizations. *Nonprofit Management and Leadership* 7: 387–403.

Simon, H. (1945). *Administrative Behavior: A Study of Decision-Making Processes in Administrative Organizations*. New York: The Free Press.

Smiley, M. (1998). *Strategic Planning for Nonprofit Organizations*. Washington, DC: National Trust for Historic Preservation.

Smith, S. R. and Lipsky, M. (1993). *Nonprofits for Hire: The Welfare State in the Age of Contracting*. Cambridge, MA: Harvard University Press.

Sotirin, P. (1984). Organizational culture: A focus on contemporary theory/research in organizational communication. A paper presented at the 70th Annual Meeting of the Speech Communication Association, Chicago, IL, November 1–4, 1984.

Stone, M. (1989). Planning as strategy in nonprofit organizations: An exploratory study. *Nonprofit and Voluntary Sector Quarterly* 18: 297–315.

Stone, M., and Crittenden, W. (1994). A guide to strategic management literature on nonprofit organizations. *Nonprofit Management and Leadership* 4(2): 193–213.

Sugin, L. (2007). Resisting the corporatization of nonprofit governance: Transforming obedience into fidelity. *Fordham Law Review* 76: 893–927.

Sutherland, J. W. (1978). *Management Handbook for Public Administrators*. New York: Van Nostrand Reinhold.

Unterman, I., and Davis, R. H. (1982). The strategy gap in not-for-profits. *Harvard Business Review* 60(3): 30–40.

Webster, S., and Wylie, M. (1988). Strategic planning in competitive environments. *Administration in Social Work* 12(3): 25–43.

Wolch, J., and Rocha, E. (1993). Planning responses to voluntary sector crises. *Nonprofit Management and Leadership* 3(4): 25–43.

Yang, K. (2008). Examining perceived honest performance reporting by public organizations: Bureaucratic politics and organizational practice. *Journal of Public Administration Research and Theory* 19(1): 81–105.

Zammuto, R., and Krakower, J. (1991). Quantitative and qualitative studies of organizational culture. *Research in Organizational Change and Development* 5(2): 83–114.

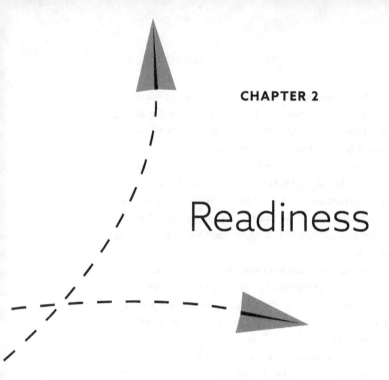

CHAPTER 2

Readiness

KEY POINTS

1. Nonprofit organizations have many reasons for strategic planning.
2. Board leadership is needed for a strategic planning process.
3. Strategic plans are generally voluntary.

Reasons for Planning

It is a strange time to be writing about strategic planning. So many nonprofit organizations are struggling with unprecedented challenges. Whether these organizations have long histories or are just getting started, they are all trying to weather the storm of a pandemic and its aftereffects, serve their missions, protect their staff and volunteers, and guide their organizations. We know some will not make it. Some will be battered but will survive, and some will be stronger. Even if organizations were formed before the previous great pandemic, the

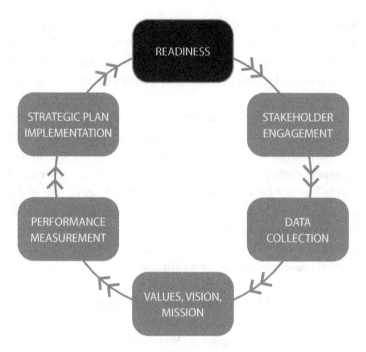

FIGURE 3
Cycle of Strategic Planning

Spanish flu in 1918, the world is a different place today. Most organizations did not have a manual for this level of disruption, although organizations have been financially shaken for many other reasons over the last 100 years, such as wars, economic depression, and political upheaval. Organizations that have come through to the other side of this pandemic are those that had planned for inevitable challenges, that are cautiously optimistic, and that are nimble enough to adjust plans as needed. If anything, this pandemic has shown me that planners do not plan because they can only envision one path forward. They plan because they are in the habit of forecasting, of thinking through scenarios. In essence, they are continuously exercising the habit of planning, so when plans need to change based on new information, they are in the best shape of their lives. I have never run a marathon, but I imagine it is the commitment to regular training that makes all the difference when you need to run 26 miles. And, if you need to run a different course or a different distance, you are ready. So yes, strategic planning is like marathon training. The more you commit to a regular schedule, the more likely you are committed to the process. It is this persistence and dedication that lead to successful strategic planning.

I have consulted with many nonprofit organizations, and one of the first things I ask is "Why do you want to do this?" I want to know the motivations behind their commitment to strategic planning because that tells me many things. It tells me whether they have asked themselves that question, thought through the implications of the process in terms of time and resources, and, overall, how much they are invested in learning about their organization and how they can improve it. Through these discussions, I find out how open they are to change. I have commented more than once:

If you want to keep doing what you are doing and how you are doing it, you don't need a strategic plan.
Just keep doing what you're doing.

If you do want to embark on a strategic planning process, you might have many reasons behind your desire. The reasons tend to boil down to internal and external pressures. Internally, a change in board or staff leadership often triggers a strategic planning process. There could also be external reasons coming from funders, donors, partners, or accrediting bodies. Many funders recommend or even require attaching strategic plans to grant requests. Nonprofit accreditation can also drive the motivation for strategic planning; for example, the Joint Commission accredits many types of health care organizations, from hospitals to nursing homes. Or an organization can pursue strategic planning to adhere to best practices or independent accreditation, such as from the Standards for Excellence Institute. A current strategic plan and monitoring of that plan is a signal to external stakeholders that the organization takes planning seriously, which means it is likely committed to best practices in other areas as well, such as financial management. This commitment gives external stakeholders some assurance that the organization is being managed and led well.

From a regulation perspective, strategic plans are a voluntary type of reporting done by nonprofits. Figure 4 depicts the various types of reporting that nonprofit organizations are required to do or voluntarily do. There are few mandatory reports, especially for external audiences (upper left corner), and even those reports are limited to nonprofits of a certain size and vary by state. I placed performance/data reports at the center of the figure since they are sometimes required, in the case of grant reports, and other times they are voluntary. They may also be used strictly for internal purposes, like staff tracking an individual client's progress, or for external purposes, such as monitoring overall participation rates. While desirable, strategic plans are voluntary (falling to the right of the vertical axis of the figure below) and are for internal as well as external audiences (above and below the horizontal axis).

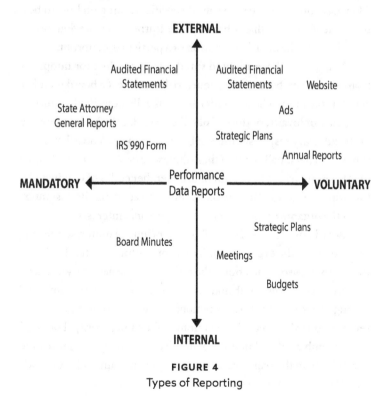

FIGURE 4
Types of Reporting

Board Leadership

It is the board's responsibility to determine the mission of the non-profit organization and ensure adequate resources to carry out that mission; this obligation is known as their fiduciary responsibility. Boards act as stewards or caretakers of an organization. While some boards are founding boards, meaning they were part of the organization's founding, the vast majority of boards are made up of volunteers who lead the organization for a while and then hand off that stewardship to the next board. They do this without receiving any personal financial benefit, which would be typical in a business setting, where board members might be reimbursed with stock, for example. Nonprofit organizations are not owned but are rather held in the public trust. Nonprofit board members volunteer to lead organizations because of their connection to the specific mission. They have not necessarily received specific training on how to be a board member other than what they have learned from previous board experience or the board orientation of a particular nonprofit.

Many states have adopted standards of conduct for nonprofit boards that have been used in court to determine if a board member acted improperly. These standards are usually described as duty of care, duty of loyalty, or duty of obedience under the broad umbrella of the fiduciary responsibilities of board members. A board member can be held personally liable if these duties are breached. BoardSource (2018) summarized nonprofit board member codes of conduct. All the responsibilities of a board come down to acting in the best interest of the organization rather than any personal interests.

Board governance responsibilities include planning so that the focus stays on the organization's mission. Volunteers tend to be attracted to stable organizations, those that have the necessary financial resources, consistent staff, and a good reputation in the community, among other factors. Board members generally are not looking to serve on boards where there is upheaval or uncertainty. Potential board members likely know this kind of situation may take more time to resolve than they can give, or it may require certain skills or knowledge they may not possess.

➤ case example #2

Before beginning a strategic planning process, I review the organization's governing documents, specifically their bylaws. I also check how frequently they have reviewed or updated their bylaws. In terms of content, I look for signs of solid leadership such as formal rules for board meetings, board terms, board composition, voting, and so on. During my review for a particular organization, I came across a term that I don't see very often, a board position referred to as "emeritus board member." Emeritus board positions are typically honorary positions meant to signal that this individual has provided exceptional leadership or service to the organization. In this instance, the emeritus board members were the two founders of the organization. While the bylaws stipulated that they no longer had a vote in board decisions, they were to receive all board communications, board meeting agendas and minutes, and could attend any board meeting. They did not have a vote in decisions, but they could speak out, and they did, to express their opinion either for or against any proposal that came before the board. This seemed to make board members uncomfortable if they voted against a certain proposal that the emeritus board members supported or vice versa. In fact, recently a new board member decided to leave after only a few months because of how heated the meetings would get when the emeritus board members were present. After I reviewed their bylaws and heard these comments from board members, we decided to postpone a formal strategic planning process until we could reconcile the seemingly powerful emeritus board members with the other board members. The planning process resumed about a year later, and the bylaws were revised to remove language allowing emeritus board member participation in meetings and other areas of influence.

⅄

What do we know about board members' evaluations of their ability to lead organizations? Gazley and Bowers (2013) studied board governance practices in nonprofit associations. Over 1,500 board members were asked to rate their board on several dimensions. About one quarter of respondents rated their board as excellent when it came to thinking strategically, but 38% thought their board needed improvement in this area. When asked whether their board achieved strategic plan goals, 31% rated their board as excellent and 24% indicated their board needed improvement. This study looked at many other elements related to strategic planning, including board performance standards (just 7% were rated excellent) and alignment of resources with strategic needs (28% were rated excellent).

Strategic planning that is done well is meant to question assumptions, seek evidence for decision-making, gain buy-in from all stakeholders, and chart a course for the future that is subject to change. Sometimes this approach requires small changes and other times more radical changes or even transformational changes. Transformational change is defined as broad and significant change to everything from culture to leadership and mission (Jick 1993). But all change is difficult. Organizations are made up of people who generally like predictability and equilibrium. Change may be generated at the top of the organization, but it does filter down and out, bumping into tension as it goes. Research suggests that change is a process of planning that needs to include information gathering, diagnosis of problems, and learning with sufficient support and resources (Balogun and Hailey 2008).

➤ case example #3

Often nonprofit organizations are formed because of a personal connection to or passion for a mission. Unfortunately there is very little support available for new organizations, and often they're started without much forethought about the longer-term work required to run a nonprofit, usually in addition to the founder's regular job, and the impact these commitments can have on personal finances and free time. Founders may also think of their nonprofit organization as a personal legacy or something to honor someone living or deceased, something to keep a person's memory alive. One nonprofit founder began with large goals, specifically to buy space within the first two years of operation so the organization could serve residents beyond the local community. Currently the organization was providing needed services using rented or free space. But demand was growing as the program's reputation increased, and the founders needed guidance to determine how to focus their time and resources. Should they purchase a building, rent a building, or set up formal lease agreements with multiple sites to continue their work? They were at a crossroads and thought a strategic plan would help give them a solid direction. After working through a process and engaging with their clients, volunteers, and board, they decided to focus on the most cost-effective service delivery they could provide at this time, which meant using publicly available space to hold their programs—at least for the next three years, at which point they would reevaluate. Thinking small is hard to do for many nonprofit start-ups, but having reasonable expectations will allow the organization to thoughtfully grow over time.

The board has the ultimate authority over and responsibility for the organization. The board must therefore support a regular examination of how the organization is doing and where it wants to be in the future. To do this, there must be a willingness to open the organization to examination, even to critique. There needs to be a willingness to accept the risk that comes with this choice. This willingness is what determines whether nonprofit organizations will do okay or, in the words of Jim Collins (2005), go from "good to great." Many founders have missed the message that Collins was trying to relay, which is that nonprofit organizations are much more difficult to run than businesses. Nonprofits actually face greater risks than businesses because, in many cases, they're using donated or contractual dollars to provide necessary public services. So nonprofit boards do need to accept a certain degree of risk in their operations, and one of those risks is to have an open and honest evaluation of how the organization is doing on a regular basis. In chapter 5, I go into detail about why and how performance measurement is a key component of the strategic planning process.

There are several resources for boards who want to support a strategic planning process. BoardSource is a membership-based organization offering resources on all kinds of issues affecting nonprofit boards, from general roles and responsibilities to fundraising, advocacy, board-staff relations, board meetings, executive evaluation, and much more. Their Board Support Program includes a board self-assessment and other educational resources and tools. They have several publications related to nonprofit strategic planning. Some resources are accessible only to members, while others are available for purchase. They offer short and economical guides such as their strategic planning guide. BoardSource also has a network of independent and affiliated consultants across the country. Membership in BoardSource is based on an organization's annual revenue, starting at $500 for organizations with less than $250,000 annual revenue. BoardSource has also produced the *Leading with Intent* research about trends in nonprofit board leadership practices and composition annually since 2014.

Nonprofit organizations have different types of boards for different reasons at different states of their evolution or organizational life cycle (Brothers and Sherman 2012). According to the Urban Institute (2018), the over 1.5 million registered nonprofits can be classified by their budget size into four broad categories. About a third of all nonprofits are very small, with less than $100,000 in annual revenue, and these are typically the "founding board" or small community organizations run entirely by volunteers. Newly formed or forming organizations have a strong passion but few policies and procedures in place. They have not yet proven their value or effectiveness. Their boards tend to be made up of direct acquaintances of the founding members who were possibly recruited for their expertise on boards or particular backgrounds, such as legal or financial. They may not have ever served on a nonprofit board and draw most of their knowledge from experiences in the private sector or other boards. They may not have any strategic planning background in nonprofit organizations. These new boards are also resistant to having a clear plan because the organization is still changing.

About another third of nonprofits have an operating budget between $100,000 and $500,000, and they have hired their first staff member or members (2018). The organization still uses volunteers extensively. More mature organizations, slightly older, are likely experiencing growth. They tend to be overly ambitious, attracted to new initiatives, and do not want to close any doors too quickly. This is a perfect time to make a simple strategic plan, which builds good planning habits as the organization grows and becomes more complex. The challenge at this point is to "right-size" the plan given the likely heavy reliance on volunteers and limited staff. Plans developed at this stage tend to be ambitious and may lack clear performance measures.

Another quarter of nonprofits have budgets between $500,000 and $5 million (2018). They have a large and professional staff with professional policies and procedures. As the organization continues to evolve, the nonprofit may stabilize, programs become more established, and the organization builds name recognition and reputation. There are also sufficient and qualified staff to carry out the day-to-day operations of the organization, and the board moves to more of a policy and fundraising position and away from direct service delivery and support. This is a time when the organization is more likely to have formal processes and practices in place, making strategic planning more routine and acceptable.

The final category contains the fewest nonprofits—those with annual revenue of over $5 million, making up about 8.5% of all nonprofits (2018). These are typically national organizations with a long history and large endowments; they're also more likely to be in the education or health-care fields. At this stage, these nonprofits have plateaued, are in decline, or are trying to revitalize. Strategic planning is a perfect way to figure out a path forward. No matter where the nonprofit is in the organizational life cycle, it can benefit from a strategic planning process, but life cycle does play a role in what that looks like, who is involved, and how ambitious the plan is.

Staff Buy-In

Often strategic planning is initiated by the board, but the impetus can also come from staff. Perhaps there is a new executive director at the helm or other leadership changes, so staff may feel that a new strategic plan is needed. Another possibility is that a funder, such as a foundation, requests a current strategic plan for the nonprofit to be eligible for funding. Whatever the initial reason, the staff and the board need to work together to decide on a strategic planning process. Senior staff should be involved throughout the process, but middle and frontline staff should certainly understand what is taking place and have the opportunity to participate. There is nothing worse than a strategic plan simply being announced to staff. This approach will not only kill morale, but it will also guarantee failure for the plan's implementation.

Ideally all staff is engaged in the process. This is critical for those staff who will be tasked with carrying out the plan, collecting data, and reporting on progress. Measuring, which will be covered more in-depth in a subsequent chapter, needs to be integral to the goal creation and plan implementation. If measures related to efficiency or effectiveness are going to be taken, then staff need to be engaged in the process so they are part of the goal creation itself. Very few nonprofit organizations have staff dedicated to data collection and analysis. It is most likely the program staff who will carry out the plan and collect the data. The data need to be integral to their work, or very little attention will be paid to the results, creating wasted time or cynicism about the process itself. Strategic planning requires champions at all levels if it is to be considered a worthy endeavor.

The planning process needs to be transparent from the initiation of the process through to measuring its success. This can be done in a variety of ways, from regular staff meetings to staff retreats, regular staff emails or newsletters, or simply conversations between supervisors and staff to reiterate the importance of the process and the plan. A strategic plan can be very motivational for staff, especially for nonprofit staff who often struggle with the ever-increasing demand for services and the limited time to deliver those services. Clear priorities can actually reduce staff stress and workload, so they feel they are actually making a difference rather than spinning in too many directions. Burnout is real, and a good strategic plan can help staff focus their energy and time.

Readiness Assessment

It is important that the board and staff go through a strategic planning readiness assessment. This can be an online survey, or part of a staff meeting or board retreat. Organizations want to make sure to ask some critical questions before beginning a readiness assessment. The organization will gain valuable insight about any potential problems, and the results can be shared with the strategic planning consultant if the organization decides to go that route. There is a readiness assessment in appendix A that asks questions about three areas: organizational understanding, leadership, and budget (Bryson 2011).

- *Organizational Understanding*: These questions ask respondents about whether the organization has a clear mission, whether people in the organization understand the mission, and whether the organization knows its stakeholders, has a clear understanding of its strengths and weaknesses, and understands the organizational culture and values.
- *Leadership*: These questions are about who will lead the strategic planning effort, whether they are capable of managing the process, whether the board works effectively on planning, whether the board has or could develop a process to include the organization's stakeholders, and whether the organization has a process or ways to effectively reach the stakeholders.
- *Budget*: These questions are about how the planning process and the key strategies will be funded, whether there are incentives for accomplishing goals, and whether there are sufficient funds to support the strategic planning process.

Based on the person's answers to these questions, the organization can determine whether it wants to proceed with the strategic planning process now, figure out whether and how to make changes before embarking on a strategic planning process, or postpone the process. Organizations may decide—and many have that I've worked with— that the time is not right to proceed. Most often, they've felt that they needed to do a little more work getting the organization ready, so they paused the process. Once the organization is ready to move forward, the next decision is to determine whether the organization would like to use a consultant or not and, if so, for what portions of the process.

Using Consultants

Strategic planning is a time to dig in to all the nooks and crannies of the organization, to cast a critical eye on what the organization is doing well and not as well.

I am often asked, "Do I need a consultant for a strategic planning process?" The simple answer is no, but you should understand the pros and cons of working with a consultant before you make that decision. There are two big factors to consider:

1. Do you have the necessary staff expertise to dedicate to strategic planning?
2. Do you have the financial resources?

Staff Expertise

If a consultant is not brought in, the nonprofit staff should have a wide variety of skills and backgrounds and include someone who could lead the strategic planning effort. The lead person does not have to be the executive director, CEO, or president, but it typically is. Another question to consider is whether this staff person is too close to the situation, making them unable to fully participate in the process and lead it at the same time. The board should look for a critical and neutral person to lead the effort, so it will receive all the information it needs to move forward. If the person leading the effort is a staff member with a long tenure, they may not be seen as impartial or they may have blind spots in the process—two limitations that should be avoided. As noted earlier, a strategic planning process is a time to dig in to all the nooks and crannies of the organization, to cast a critical eye on what the organization is doing well and not as well. Many boards feel more confident when someone from the outside affirms what staff is telling them. This validation is often unspoken, but the staff knows that no matter how many times they have said something is a problem, nothing might happen until someone from outside the organization confirms it. It is our instinct to advocate for the programs and services we feel are important, have helped to start, or deliver ourselves. Nonprofit staff are also very protective of their coworkers because they know they work hard and everyone sees the benefits every day. It can be difficult to ask questions such as "Are the programs we offer in this area providing the best service to our clients?" or "Is our organization the best at delivering this service compared to other programs in our area?" These are tough questions, and they should be asked during a strategic planning process. I have generally found that someone from outside of the organization will be less biased in this situation, leading the conversations to be less confrontational.

Financial Resources

If the nonprofit determines it will need to bring in an outside consultant, the top priority is to think through possible sources to pay for these services. Foundations may have special funding available for capacity building or strategic planning work. Start with your local community foundation. The Council on Foundations (n.d.) offers an online locator for community foundations across the United States. Community Foundations of Canada also offers a locator of community foundations in that country. Funding for strategic planning is often lumped with capacity-building grants targeted to increasing the strength of nonprofit organizations to improve their planning and systems. For example, the Ausherman Family Foundation (2020) offers capacity-building grants for this purpose. So, in terms of a strategy, if you are looking for external funds, start with your local community foundation, then determine if any of your local family foundations fund capacity building.

If there are no external funds available, you have options from your existing funds. You can build the cost of an external consultant into your operating budget for an upcoming year. Unless your budget is growing, this means you will have to reduce funding for something else, which may be problematic. You can raise new funds with a specific appeal, starting with your board of directors. This is a desirable way to also demonstrate the board's commitment to strategic planning and avoids placing an additional financial burden on the executive director to allocate existing dollars from a finite budget. A final option is to draw financial resources from existing savings or reserves. This is also preferable to using existing budgeted resources. Of course, if savings or reserves are already low, this may not be the way to go.

There is no standard consulting fee for strategic planning, but some general guidelines are useful. Consultants range from a one-person shop to a large consulting firm, with everything in between. You will likely know of some consultants in your area. Your first task is to draft a request for proposal (RFP). This document will outline what the ideal scope of work is and will give the consultant a clear picture of your expectations. Since this type of consulting is generally based on how many hours will be spent working on the project, you will want to be as clear as possible so the consultant can estimate the time involved. In appendix B, I've included a request for proposal for the strategic planning process and facilitation for the St. Charles Public Library District. Because the library district is a government entity, this RFP was circulated publicly. Nonprofit organizations do not have to circulate their RFPs publicly, but the outline is useful since it is very clear about what the expectations for a consultant are. The RFP also includes a clear timeline, which is useful for consultants as they consider their other commitments.

The size of the project will also likely inform what kinds of consultants are interested in the project. Small budgets will likely interest individual consultants or small consulting firms. If you need help identifying nonprofit consultants to send your RFP to, start with your state nonprofit association. They will usually have a list of members who are also nonprofit consultants. Our state nonprofit association in Illinois, Forefront, also has its consulting enterprise called Converge Consulting. The Association of Consultants to Nonprofits (ACN), a nationwide community of nonprofit consultants (2019), maintains a searchable consultant database. The Grand Victoria Foundation (2006) put together a guide for nonprofits that use consultants. Another option is to reach out to the Taproot Foundation, which matches nonprofits with pro bono assistance from skilled volunteers. Taproot (2021) has a number of resources, webinars, and publications available free of charge on their website. You could also reach out to your local community college and university to see if they have any faculty engaged in this type of work, and they may be able to provide some assistance, depending on the size of the project. They may be able to enlist the help of students as part of a class project, for example, conducting research on your clients or market research. There are also some units on college and university campuses that engage directly in consulting with nonprofits for a fee. Start with your local college or university to see if they have a professional-development or outreach center. Even if they cost money, consulting services from a college or university are generally subsidized to some degree, so you wouldn't be paying for all the associated costs generally included by private consulting firms. Again, who is interested will depend on the scope of work and the timeline given in your RFP, so spend the necessary time to think that through first.

The Process

Whether you lead the planning process internally or use a consultant, the nonprofit organization should have a structure in place to carry it out. You will need to determine whether the whole board will be involved, which makes sense if your board is a reasonable size. But if you have a large board, over 20 people, then you may want to create a subcommittee or task force to divide responsibilities and consider how or whether the whole board will engage in the process. The executive committee of the board (president, vice president, secretary, treasurer) may want to draft the RFP, which will be circulated to the full board for comment. This smaller group of individuals can be primarily responsible, but a broader buy-in early in the process will likely lead to better participation in the process and certainly better implementation. Ideally the smaller group, the strategic planning task force, could be a mix of board and senior staff so both groups feel engaged in the process and responsible to make sure it is carried out. A consultant may also advise the organization on how best to create the task force or subcommittee based on their previous work with non-profit organizations.

In addition to having a clear and thought-out RFP for consulting services, you will need to create criteria or a rubric to evaluate the proposals. You'll also want to make sure the individual or firm making a proposal to you meets the minimum requirements, and you'll want to understand what their specific experience is in working with nonprofit organizations. You may have some strategic planning consultants respond who have only worked with private businesses. While they may have good facilitation skills and can build consensus in a team, they may not understand the terminology and context of the nonprofit sector. Also, nonprofit governance with a volunteer board of directors is not the same thing as ownership in the private sector. It is much more nuanced and comes with different expectations of accountability and transparency. Ask the consultant for client references from their nonprofit work to get specific feedback about the consultant's process and their experience working with nonprofit boards. Nonprofit consultants doing strategic planning tend to be good generalists. They understand the various aspects of board governance, staff relations, marketing and communications, fundraising, program development, financial management, and more. Some nonprofit consultants have specific experience, for example as fundraising consultants, that you may need if your strategic plan goals involve a capital campaign. But most nonprofits are well served by a generalist leading a strategic planning effort because of the broad array of subjects and issues that can arise inside and outside the organization.

While an organization can use a consultant to assist with the strategic planning process, it is important that the final plan be written by the board or staff person leading the effort. A consultant may draft the big ideas, but the plan should be written so it will ultimately connect to annual work plans and performance measures that the board and staff find more useful. A written strategic plan may be perfectly correct in tone and structure, yet it may not be workable or may be overly ambitious for the organization at the current time. The last thing you want is a beautiful document that took so much time, money, and effort to go unused or not to be valued as a true planning document.

Timing

To complete your RFP, you'll want to think about when you'd like to have a finished strategic plan. Then the work really begins! Timing is an important element of the process. Is there a naturally slower period in your organization that you could take advantage of and fill with strategic planning? Maybe your organization mainly serves students, so summer might make sense. You have to think about when staff will have the energy and time to participate but also when your board is likely able to dedicate the time. You will want to generally stay away from the traditional holiday period of mid-November through early January. Also, you may want to consider your fiscal year. Maybe you want to kick off your new strategic plan at the beginning of your next fiscal year. If that is July 1, you can start the process in January and have goals ready to discuss concerning setting your next year's budget (see chapter 7). There is no such thing as perfect timing because there will always be some conflicts, but the issue makes a good discussion to have with the board and staff, if only to think through potentially ideal timing. Depending on the strategic planning process your board adopts, the time frame could be a few weeks, with only one board retreat and then writing the plan; or you could gather significant data about the organization, engage with different kinds of stakeholders over several months, conduct broader community meetings, have several staff and board meetings, and then develop the plan itself. I suggest that if you have never carried out a more elaborate process, do so now and use this opportunity to create a baseline for your organization, so you know exactly where you are starting from, and then you can carry out more scaled-down versions in subsequent years.

DISCUSSION QUESTIONS

1. Why should nonprofit boards and staff work together on a strategic plan?
2. Why would foundations and other funders ask for a nonprofit's strategic plan?
3. What are the benefits and drawbacks of using an outside consultant for strategic planning assistance?

REFERENCES

Association of Consultants to Nonprofits. (2019). Directory. https://www.acnconsult.org/Find-a-Consultant.

Ausherman Family Foundation. (2020). Capacity building grant updates. Accessed July 24, 2020. https://www.aushermanfamilyfoundation.org/capacity-building-grant-updates/.

Balogun, J., and Hailey, V. H., eds. (2008). *Exploring Strategic Change*. Hoboken, NJ: Pearson Education.

BoardSource. (2018). Nonprofit board member code of conduct and ethics. https://boardsource.org/code-of-conduct-and-ethics/.

Brothers, J., and Sherman, A. (2012). *Building Nonprofit Capacity: A Guide to Managing Change through Organizational Lifecycles*. Independence, KY: John Wiley & Sons.

Collins, J. (2001). *Good to Great: Why Some Companies Make the Leap and Others Don't*. New York: Harper Business.

Collins, J. (2005). *Good to Great and the Social Sectors: Why Business Thinking Is Not the Answer*. New York: Harper Collins.

Community Foundations of Canada. (n.d.). Local community foundations. Accessed February 22, 2022. https://communityfoundations.ca/find-a-community-foundation/.

Converge Consulting. (n.d.). (Website). Accessed February 22, 2022. https://weconverge.org/.

Council on Foundations. (n.d.). Community foundation locator. Council on Foundations. Accessed December 14, 2020. https://www.cof.org/page/community-foundation-locator.

Gazley, B., and Bowers, A. (2013). *What makes high performing boards: Effective governance practices in member-serving organizations*. Washington, DC: ASAE Foundation.

Grand Victoria Foundation. (2006). The insider's guide to outside advice: A toolkit. https://marillacmissionfund.org/application/files/3915/6467/8875/Grand_Victoria__insidersguide_2006.pdf.

Jick, T., ed. (1993). *Managing Change: Cases and Concepts*. New York: Irwin McGraw-Hill.

Joint Commission. (n.d.). (Website). Accessed February 20, 2022. https://www.jointcommission.org/.

Leading with Intent. (n.d.). BoardSource: Index of nonprofit board practices. Leading with intent. Accessed February 20, 2022. https://leadingwithintent.org/.

Standards for Excellence Institute. (n.d.). (Website). Accessed February 20, 2022. https://standardsforexcellence.org/.

Taproot Foundation. (n.d.). (Website). Accessed March 17, 2021. https://taprootfoundation.org/.

Urban Institute. (2018). The nonprofit sector in brief: Public charities, giving, and volunteering. https://nccs.urban.org/publication/nonprofit -sector-brief-2018#size.

CHAPTER 3

Stakeholder Engagement

KEY POINTS

1. How are stakeholders in businesses different from those in nonprofit organizations?
2. How do nonprofit organizations identify their stakeholders?
3. What are some ways to engage stakeholders in the strategic planning process?

What Does the Research Say?

In the nonprofit literature, stakeholders are defined in several ways. A stakeholder can be anyone or any group that has a "stake" in what the organization does; meaning, "any person or group that is able to make a claim on an organization's attention, resources, or output or who may be affected by the organization" (Lewis 2001, 202). Nonprofit organizations have many stakeholders, such as funders, referral agencies, community organizations, donors, government units,

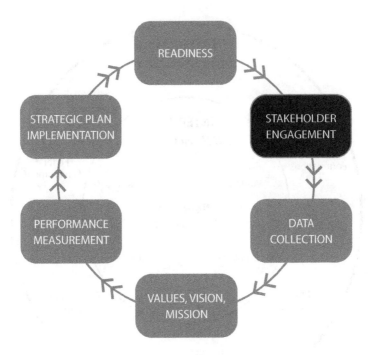

FIGURE 5
Cycle of Strategic Planning

volunteers, clients or members, staff, and board members (Van 1994). These relationships are critical to an organization's mission and must be managed well (Ospina, Diaz, and O'Sullivan 2002; Herman and Renz 1997; Tschirhart 1996; Bigelow and Stone 1995; D'Aunno, Sutton, and Price 1991). It is essential for nonprofits to have positive relationships with their stakeholders for legitimacy and accountability, which requires two-way communication (Ospina, Diaz, and O'Sullivan 2002; Drucker 1990). Furthermore, nonprofit stakeholders are connected to each other, so the nonprofit must take care to have consistency across stakeholder groups (Balser and McClusky 2005). Identifying who the stakeholders are and how, when, and why they should be involved are key strategic choices to make during stakeholder analyses.

To identify stakeholders, first consider what individuals or groups depend on the nonprofit organization for services. The

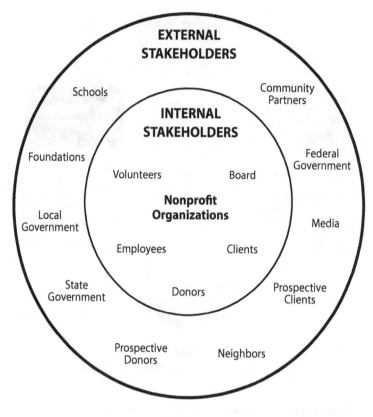

FIGURE 6
Various Nonprofit Stakeholders

stakeholders can be clients or members, for example. Nonprofit organizations are founded and controlled primarily by those stakeholders who personally benefit from the organization's services or those who fund the organization's services for the benefit of others (such as donors). This contrasts with private-sector shareholders, who are interested in financial returns (Ben-Ner and Van Hoomissen 1991). Nonprofit organizations can act as contractual agents for governments, contract with businesses to provide services, partner with governments and businesses, create for-profit entities separate from their nonprofit mission, operate as a nonprofit affiliate of a for-profit company or a nonprofit trade association, partner with governments and for-profit businesses on payroll deduction plans or other fund-raising campaigns, and have volunteers from the corporate and government sectors (Young and Steinberg 1995).

Because of the expansive roles and types of nonprofit organizations, stakeholders in them can also be defined by larger webs than stakeholders in businesses. Abzug and Webb (1999) suggested categorizing nonprofit stakeholders into the following groups: community, competitors, customers, employees, governments, stockholders, and suppliers. Community stakeholder groups refer to community-interest groups that may be working with or against a nonprofit organization on a specific issue. The competitor group refers to other nonprofit organizations that provide the same services. The customer stakeholder group means nonprofits purchase goods and services individually or as a group, such as the purchase of legal services or even office supplies. Employees are stakeholders, especially when they organize into a union or professional association. Nonprofit organizations also have governments as a stakeholder group since they work with or for governments. Nonprofits are stockholders since they manage their endowments or pension funds with stock holdings. Finally, nonprofits have stakeholders connected to supplying services to businesses through contracting, such as medical or educational services. They might also supply labor for various public programs (1999).

Another way to identify stakeholders is to look at the degree to which the nonprofit is dependent on others, such as funders and donors. These are individuals or agencies that do not receive the services directly but instead financially support the delivery of those services to others. Researchers have combined agency theory with stewardship to express the differences in approaches to stakeholder identification and relationship management. Agency theory relies more heavily on the financial relationship or position of control and, therefore, has stronger accountability requirements. Stewardship theory, in contrast, is focused on the relationship and based more in sociological or psychological terms: collaboration occurs because of high trust and intrinsic reward in working together (Sundaramurthy and Lewis 2003; Davis, Schoorman, and Donaldson 1997).

Combining principal-agent theory and stakeholder theory, re-searchers have classified principal-agent relationships into different categories (Van Puyvelde et al. 2012).

Defining Stakeholders

Since nonprofit organizations are not operated for personal financial gain, there are no shareholders. Instead, board members act in the public interest as "trustees." Some argue that board members act as principals, and nonprofit staff act as agents, but others argue that boards do not necessarily control the work of staff, which agency theory implies. Instead, boards act as stewards for the organization, and board members and staff act cohesively to fulfill the organization's mission, adhering to more of a stewardship-theory perspective (Van Puyvelde et al. 2012).

Governance is the process by which constituency voices are brought into the organization, traditionally through community representatives on the board. Board members are important stakeholders given their connection to the community, especially if they seek to be representative of that community. We do know, however, that boards struggle with being truly representative of the community given their emphasis on financial contributions (Chaskin 2003). Stakeholder engagement does strengthen legitimacy (Leardini, Moggi, and Rossi 2018).

Because of the involvement of multiple stakeholder groups, nonprofit organizations often face challenges in managing all those relationships. Nonprofits, while focused on their missions, tend to struggle to include those they serve in strategic planning. Nonprofit organizations, however, must understand the needs of the people they serve, since demand should influence the supply of services (Gazley and Guo 2020). Some nonprofits do spend more time managing their funding relationships at the expense of client-related activities, especially those nonprofits that are more financially dependent on corporate donors, if the board does not match the clientele served, and if the board is dominated by more affluent individuals (Alexander and Nank 2009). Research suggests that stakeholders are interested in knowing how the organization is doing. Nonprofits that engaged with the people they serve were able to set organizational priorities and negotiate accountability (Ospina, Diaz, and O'Sullivan 2002). In a study of youth homes, the adolescents and their families wanted to be involved at the operational level and the policy level of the organization. The researchers used Arnstein's participation ladder (1969) and found that stakeholder engagement would necessarily lead to co-decision-making. Co-decision-making requires the organization to give up control, not just delegate specific power, and rely on trust to address issues (Fassin et al. 2017).

When a nonprofit engages stakeholders in decision-making, the nonprofit becomes more responsive to external needs, and the organization is legitimized. Legitimacy is certainly subjective, and when it exists, it links the value of the organization to the larger system of which it is a part (Lindblom 1994). All nonprofits struggle with legitimacy, particularly new ones. Nonprofit boards must create the proper mechanisms to make sure that the nonprofit's stakeholders are not only aware of the nonprofit but understand the value it brings to the community (Leardini, Moggi, and Rossi 2018). While shared values with stakeholders may help secure their support (Dart 2004), all nonprofits want to demonstrate that they are serving a true community need (Guo and Musso 2007).

Donors are part of a principal-agent relationship supported by nonprofit financial reporting (where donors can find out whether their donated dollars are being spent wisely). A stewardship-based approach means both the nonprofit and the donor are operating in a high-trust environment with mutual respect and reciprocity. Stewardship is a critical component of the fundraising process (Van Puyvelde et al. 2012). Some research suggests that donors make up a key stakeholder group and that donor satisfaction is a key measure of that relationship. Donor loyalty to the organization is positively affected by service quality and organizational identification (Leipnitz 2014; Arnstein 1969). Donor satisfaction occurs when the donor's prior expectations are met with actual performance and the donor personally identifies with the organization's mission: they see themselves as part of that mission (Leipnitz 2014; Arnstein 1969). Recent research suggests that as nonprofits rely on external donations from private sources, long-term innovation declines. When a nonprofit focuses on building long-term relationships with donors, however, innovation increases (Ranucci and Lee 2019).

Another nonprofit stakeholder is a foundation. Private foundations can be independent, family, or corporate foundations such as the Ford Foundation or the Target Foundation. There are about 73,000 private foundations in the United States (Council on Foundations 2021). Public foundations are not easily classified, but they do dedicate a significant portion of their annual budgets to grant making (2021). One example of a public foundation is a community foundation. Community foundations assure management of charitable donations in perpetuity. The original concept was "a partnership of expertness between the banks and citizen leaders" (National Council on Community Foundations 1961, 9). Funds are gathered through direct gifts, solicitation, grants, or bequests, and are then held in trust for the greater common good as determined by the trustees of the foundation. The Council on Foundations (1999) estimated that community foundations served 86% of the US population and continued to grow steadily. Even among foundations, community foundations are unique in their donor base, their geographic emphasis, and the fact that they must still maintain their 501(c)(3) status as a public charity.

In terms of historical development, community foundations grew tremendously from 1914 to 1930 and were primarily established by bankers. The first community foundation was founded in Cleveland, Ohio, on January 2, 1914. After the Depression and up to the end of World War II, however, interest in community foundations leveled off. The post-war era broadened interest in community foundations beyond bankers. They grew rapidly in large cities as well as smaller rural areas across the country. In 1969 community foundations were given the preferred tax status of public charities under the Tax Reform Act. According to the Foundation Center, there were 328 community foundations in 1990. Based on the National Center for Charitable Statistics for 2008, there were 2,235 community foundations (identified by the T31 Community Foundation designation using the

National Taxonomy of Exempt Entities). Community foundations have also expanded around the globe, particularly in Europe, although numbers are also starting to grow in Africa and Asia.

Foundations, especially community foundations, are an example of place-based philanthropy because they typically concentrate their funding in a geographic region or regions. Since the 1980s, foundations have been partners in local neighborhood revitalization and community development (Stone 2015). Foundations can be part of network governance, where different groups are engaged to address larger place-based issues. They may convene groups to address an issue and fund the nonprofits addressing that issue. In a study of the role of private foundations in neighborhood revitalization, philanthropic foundations were an important source of funding and support for neighborhood-based organizations in Cleveland and Baltimore, and they contributed to the creation of neighborhood-development policies in those cities as well (Pill 2019). There are power dynamics to be aware of, however, when it comes to foundations and the organizations they fund, and foundations can drive community priorities through their funding guidelines and support.

Government can also be an important stakeholder in a nonprofit, particularly in those that are dependent on government grants or contracts for funding. A great deal of research has been done on resource dependency theory (RDT), beginning with Pfeffer and Salancik's book (1978). Over time, RDT "has become one of the most influential theories in organizational theory and strategic management" (Hillman, Withers, and Collins 2009). RDT acknowledges the influence of the external environment on organizational behavior. The organization can act to reduce the power of that influence and control over vital resources, however, by attempting to increase its own power in five general areas: mergers or vertical integration, joint ventures, boards of directors, political action, and executive succession (Pfeffer and Salancik 1978). In the case of government funding, as funding reliance increases, the community connection becomes weaker (Guo 2007).

There are three resource dependence criteria or dimensions of dependence: the importance of the resource, the availability of alternatives, and the ability to compel provision of the resource (Bacharach and Lawler 1981). Resource dependency leads to interdependence of nonprofit and public organizations (Saidel 1991). Because of the perception that resource dependency is not desirable, a common tactic to protect against it is revenue diversification. Overall revenue diversification may increase the financial stability of these nonprofits, especially by "equalizing their reliance on earned income, investments, and contributions" (Carroll and Stater 2008). Organizations that rely on any one source of revenue are more likely to experience revenue volatility.

Many frameworks seek to explain the relationship between government and nonprofit organizations, such as the public-service framework, the co-creation framework, the advocate-provider framework and the co-governance framework (Denhardt and Denhardt n.d.; Cheng 2019; Torfing, Sorensen, and Roiseland 2019; Fyall 2017; Pestoff, Osborne, and Brandsen 2016). Another theory that helps to explain the complex government-nonprofit relationship is principal-agent theory. Principal-agent theory suggests that when "activities are too costly or too complex to be provided by one principal, . . . a principal hires an agent with the knowledge and skills" needed to carry out those activities. A perfect example of a costly or complex field is the arts. In this case, the state is the principal, and the nonprofit organizations are the agents. The bulk of arts programming is carried out in this way in that the agents are funded either directly or indirectly by states. Actions based on the principal-agent theory, however, do complicate accountability for public funds. Certainly, you can have financial accountability, making sure that nonprofit organizations account for grant funds; that is, explaining how and for what purpose the money was spent. In essence this is procedural accountability. This work is onerous for nonprofits, particularly for small organizations who may lack sophisticated accounting and reporting technology. Another aspect of accountability is performance accountability, which aims to ensure that grant funds are spent in such a way to meet performance objectives with measurable results demonstrating effectiveness and other objectives set by the state arts council. In MacDonald's study of human-service nonprofit organizations in Australia, "doubts were raised by informants within both the funding bodies and the peak organizations about whether the departments had sufficient resources to achieve accountability" (McDonald 1997, 57). Dependence on government funding can cause cash flow interruptions, bureaucratization, or distraction from the organization's mission (Froelich 1999). Competing demands are one of the most important challenges facing nonprofit managers as they try to raise funds to carry out their missions (Miller 2002). As government funding decreases, nonprofit organizations may turn to commercial revenue generation, which then creates a "customer" orientation and a consumer stakeholder group (Eikenberry and Kluver 2004; Salamo 1999).

Since the late 1960s, public services are more likely to be provided via contracts with nonprofit organizations than by public employees, and traditional government grants to nonprofits have largely been replaced with performance contracts (Boris et al. 2010; Smith 2010; Martin 2002; Gordon 2001; Martin 2001). Because government contracts are an important source of revenue for nonprofit organizations, nonprofit agencies that have contracted with the government have increased the requirements for performance data to maintain the performance contracts (Gazley 2008). Nonprofit partners are often trusted more, screened less, monitored less, gain more discretion, and are awarded longer contracts than for-profit contractors, while at the same time achieving higher service quality, responsiveness to government, and customer satisfaction compared to private businesses (Witesman and Fernandez 2013). Researchers have also examined the extent of public-nonprofit partnerships in many areas, such as emergency management (Kapucu 2006), nonprofit neighborhood organizations (Chaskin and Greenberg 2015), community-based nonprofit organizations (Alexander and Nank 2009), public schools (Nelson and Gazley 2014), public libraries (Schatteman and Bingle 2015), public parks (Cheng 2018; Gazley, Cheng, and Lafontant 2018), economic development (Deslatte, Schatteman, and Stokan 2019), and human or social services (Van Slyke 2006). Because of ever-increasing financial constraints on governments and nonprofits, collaboration will likely continue, especially where they share mutual interests. Trust between collaborating agencies and organizational capacity remains important for effective partnerships between governments and nonprofits (Collins and Gerlach 2019).

But it is not just the administrative side of government that should be identified as a stakeholder. A nonprofit needs to consider elected officials. They may be the ones approving funding requests or making decisions about expansion plans. Because of the contractual relationship between governments and nonprofit organizations to deliver public services, elected officials are important stakeholders at all levels. Some nonprofit missions are also specifically focused on advocacy and policy change, so elected officials drive their behavior and are an important constituency. Some nonprofit organizations do both; they are advocates and providers (Fyall 2017). Nonprofit providers, mainly 501(c)(3) nonprofits, work for the most part with administrative officials and street-level bureaucrats—that is, frontline government workers—often due to a contractual or funding relationship. Other nonprofit organizations are purely nonprofit advocates, possibly operating under other types of charitable designations and engaging directly in the public policy process. Their stakeholders are likely politicians and public managers. While 501(c)(3) charitable organizations are restricted in some political behavior, they can and often do participate in other types of advocacy to engage in the public policy process on behalf of the people they serve.

Researchers have also studied what happens if nonprofit organizations do not manage their stakeholder relationships well. These relationships can weaken due to an organizational scandal, but nonprofits can reduce those effects by voluntarily disclosing information; however, the effects won't disappear completely (Willems and Faulk 2019). The findings also confirmed that stakeholders of nonprofit organizations are different from stakeholders of organizations in the business sector, particularly because of the nature of the work itself and the lack of publicly available performance data. Overall, greater transparency and accountability in stakeholder relationships does build trust and greater donor commitment (Becker 2018; Tremblay-Boire and Prakash 2015; Saxton, Neely, and Guo 2014; Saxton, Kuo, and Ho 2012; Cordery and Baskerville 2011; Bryce 2007; Gibelman and Gelman 2001).

In Practice

Nonprofit organizations often struggle to determine who should provide input for their planning process. Who are their major stakeholders? Outside of the board of directors, who else should be involved? There are no right or wrong answers here. Boards articulate the organization's mission, vision, and goals. Their second major function is to hold the administrative staff accountable for their performance. Therefore, by their very nature, boards constitute the single most important stakeholder in strategic plan formulation.

Staff constitute the next most important stakeholder in the planning process. Senior staff have a clear stake in organizational performance and public perception. Because administrators are intimately involved in all facets of a nonprofit's operations, they are the most likely stakeholder to identify the organization's weaknesses and strengths as well as opportunities and threats. Given their roles, administrators are likely cognizant of nuanced strategic needs for change confronting the organization in contrast to board members, who are volunteers and may not possess the technical expertise to fully comprehend certain organizational issues. Involving staff in the planning process helps to develop a better plan and encourages buy-in throughout the hierarchy (Mara 2000). Unfortunately, this is not always common practice.

➤ case example #4

A nonprofit recently elected a new board president who is eager to assist the organization and move its mission forward. He has served on the board for three years already, so he feels like he has a pretty good grasp of its challenges. He has also been part of other strategic planning processes that seemed to drag on for months and months, only to arrive where at the start again—an experience he does not wish to repeat here. He's pretty sure that the board can create a new strategic plan during a retreat, since it shouldn't take more than a few hours to come to consensus. The retreat itself is facilitated by a former board member who knows the organization. The retreat goes well, and everyone leaves energized and feeling a strong sense of accomplishment. The board releases the strategic plan to the staff a few weeks later and is surprised that the staff are not as excited as the board by this new plan. The executive director, who was the only staff member at the board retreat, shares the staff reactions to the new plan at the next board meeting. The staff feel blindsided; some programs are significantly reduced in size without clear direction about where the current program participants can go to have their needs met, while there are several new programs identified in the plan with no corresponding increase in funding. Furthermore, the new director of development is tasked with a 20% increase in overall fundraising goals without any new staff or additional resources to achieve that goal. The board realizes that maybe their focus on efficiency came at the expense of staff engagement and possibly client engagement. They decide to put off adopting the new plan and to come up with ways to get the staff involved from the beginning of the process. Lesson learned.

⋀

Looking at this case, beyond the board and staff, who should be engaged in the planning process? Again, there is no right or wrong answer; however, there is an argument to be made that the broader the engagement, the more benefits result. These include the following:

- Signaling that the organization is investing time and resources to think about its future and plan ahead
- Getting stakeholders excited about possibilities and therefore engaging them at a deeper level in the organization
- Building positive energy and enthusiasm among volunteers, staff, donors, and so on
- Focusing the efforts of staff on the big goals of the organization, which can get lost in the day-to-day management and service delivery
- Asking good questions that often people too close to the organization simply cannot think to ask, and seeing how this impartiality is critical

- Building new or solidifying existing relationships because of the genuine desire to seek out the opinions and perceptions of your stakeholders
- Building two-way communication between the organization and its stakeholders to improve the exchange of information and ideas
- Testing new ideas and solutions to funding challenges with those individuals or groups who may be part of a campaign down the road
- Collecting data (see chapter 4) from the stakeholders, which can be very useful to the process

To get the word out about the strategic planning process and how stakeholders can participate, organizations should use their existing communication channels such as their newsletters, website, and social media. They should also send out press releases to announce the planning process.

Organizations should create a map of stakeholders with the board or strategic planning committee to first identify internal and external stakeholders. They can do this with just a large piece of paper or a whiteboard. Important stakeholders are those individuals receiving the programs or services, such as clients, members, and possibly family members. Organizations should think about people who have received their services in the past as well as current participants. "Alumni" of the program are important since they received services and can evaluate the effectiveness of those programs. Asking current recipients for input can be less productive because they will be biased toward maintaining or increasing current services. Of course, their perceptions of current services are important and valid, but it is also important to gather information for strategic planning purposes from other stakeholders who may be focused on the longer term rather than the short term. See figure 7 for examples of stakeholders.

Gathering input from stakeholders validates how nonprofit organizations frame potential strategic issues. If the separate stakeholders agree on the nature of a problem, it is probably a strategic issue. Ultimately, in the majority of cases, the governing board determines the degree of end-user input into strategic plan formulation.

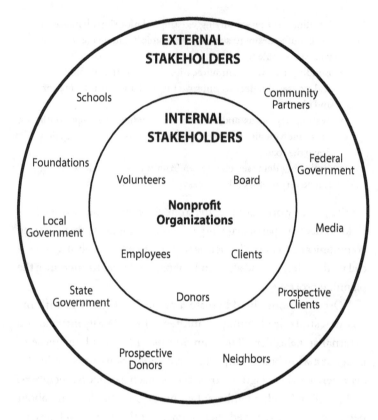

FIGURE 7
Various Nonprofit Stakeholders

DISCUSSION QUESTIONS

1. Why would a community member participate in the strategic planning process with a nonprofit organization?
2. How important is it that the board is representative of the community it seeks to serve and how does this affect strategic planning?
3. Why is it important to engage staff in the strategic planning process?
4. What are some ways the organization can communicate with its stakeholders about the strategic planning process and how they can participate?

REFERENCES

Abzug, R., and Webb, N. (1999). Relationships between nonprofit and for-profit organizations: A stakeholder perspective. *Nonprofit and Voluntary Sector Quarterly* 28(4), 416–431.

Alexander, J., and Nank, R. (2009). Public–nonprofit partnership: Realizing the new public service. *Administration & Society* 41: 364. https://doi.org/10.1177/0095399709332296.

Arnstein, S. (1969). A ladder of citizen participation. *Journal of the American Planning Association.* 35(4): 216–224.

Bacharach, S., and Lawler, J. (1981). Power and tactics in bargaining. *Industrial and Labor Relations Review* 34: 219–233.

Balser, D., and McClusky, J. (2005). Managing stakeholder relationships and nonprofit organization effectiveness. *Nonprofit Management and Leadership* 15(3): 295–315.

Becker, A. (2018). An experimental study of voluntary nonprofit accountability and effects on public trust, reputation, perceived quality, and donation behavior. *Nonprofit and Voluntary Sector Quarterly* 47(3): 562–582.

Ben-Ner, A., and Van Hoomissen, T. (1991). Nonprofit organizations in the mixed economy: A demand and supply analysis. *Annals of Public and Cooperative Economics* 62: 519–550.

Bigelow, B., and Stone, M. (1995). Why don't they do what we want? An exploration of organizational responses to institutional pressure in community health centers. *Public Administration Review* 55(2): 183–192.

Boris, E., deLeon, E., Roeger, K., and Nikolova, M. (2010). *Contracts and Grants between Human Service Nonprofits and Governments.* Washington, DC: Urban Institute, Center on Nonprofits and Philanthropy.

Bryce, H. J. (2007). The public's trust in nonprofit organizations: The role of relationship marketing and management. *California Management Review* 49(4): 112–131.

Carroll, D., and Stater, K. (2008). Revenue diversification in nonprofit organizations: Does it lead to financial stability? *Journal of Public Administration Research and Theory* 19: 947–966.

Chaskin, R. (2003). Fostering neighborhood democracy: Legitimacy and accountability within loosely coupled systems. *Nonprofit and Voluntary Sector Quarterly* 32(2): 161–189.

Chaskin, R. J., and Greenberg, D. (2015). Between public and private action: Neighborhood organizations and local governance. *Nonprofit and Voluntary Sector Quarterly* 44(2): 248–267.

Cheng, Y. (2018). Governing government-nonprofit partnerships: Linking governance mechanisms to collaboration stages. *Public Performance and Management Review* 42(1): 190–212.

Cheng, Y. (2019) Exploring the role of nonprofits in public service provision: Moving from coproduction to cogovernance. *Public Administration Review* 79(2): 203–14.

Collins, T., and Gerlach, J. D. (2019). Bridging the gaps: Local government and nonprofit collaborations. *Journal of Public and Nonprofit Affairs* 5(2): 118–133.

Cordery, C. J., and Baskerville, R. F. (2011). Charity transgressions, trust and accountability. *Voluntas: International Journal of Voluntary and Nonprofit Organizations* 22(2): 197–213.

Council on Foundations. (n.d.). Private foundations. Council on Foundations. Accessed February 20, 2022. https://www.cof.org/foundation-type /private-foundations.

Council on Foundations. (n.d.). Public foundations. Council on Foundations. Accessed February 20, 2022. https://www.cof.org/foundation -type/public-foundations.

Dart, R. (2004). The legitimacy of social enterprise. *Nonprofit Management and Leadership* 14(4): 411–424.

D'Aunno, T., Sutton, R., and Price, R. (1991). Isomorphism and external support in conflicting institutional environments: A study of drug abuse treatment units. *Academy of Management Journal* 34(3): 636–661.

Davis, J., Schoorman, F. D., and Donaldson, L. (1997). The distinctiveness of agency theory and stewardship theory. *Academy of Management Review* 22(3): 611–613;

Denhardt, R., and Denhardt, J. (n.d.) The new public service: Serving rather than steering. *Public Administration Review* 60(6): 549–559.

Deslatte, A., Schatteman, A., and Stokan, E. (2019). Handing over the keys: Local nonprofit economic development corporations and their implications for accountability and inclusion. *Public Performance and Management Review* 42(1): 90–114.

Drucker, P. (1990). *Managing the Nonprofit Organization*. New York: Harper-Collins.

Eikenberry, A., and Kluver, J. (2004). The marketization of the nonprofit sector: Civil society at risk? *Public Administration Review* 64(2): 132–140.

Fassin, Y., Deprez, J., Van den Abeele, A., and Heene, A. (2017). Complementaries between stakeholder management and participative management:

Evidence from the youth care sector. *Nonprofit and Voluntary Sector Quarterly* 46(3): 586–606.

Froelich, K. (1999). Diversification of revenue strategies: Evolving resource dependence in nonprofit organizations. *Nonprofit and Voluntary Sector Quarterly* 28(3): 232–254.

Fyall, R. (2017). Nonprofits as advocates and providers: A conceptual framework. *Policy Studies Journal* 45(1): 121–143.

Gandía, J. L. (2011). Internet disclosure by nonprofit organizations: Empirical evidence of nongovernmental organizations for development in Spain. *Nonprofit and Voluntary Sector Quarterly* 40(1): 57–78.

Gazley, B. (2008). Beyond the contract: The scope and nature of informal government-nonprofit partnerships. *Public Administration Review* 68(1): 141–154.

Gazley, B., and Guo, C. (2020). What do we know about nonprofit collaboration? A systematic review of the literature. *Nonprofit Management and Leadership* 31(2): 211–232.

Gazley, B., Cheng, Y., and Lafontant, C. (2018). Charitable support for US national and state parks through the lens of coproduction and government failure theories. *Nonprofit Policy Forum* 9(4): 20180022. https://doi.org/10.1515/npf-2018-0022.

Gibelman, M., and Gelman, S. R. (2001). Very public scandals: Nongovernmental organizations in trouble. *Voluntas: International Journal of Voluntary and Non-profit Organizations* 12(1): 49–66.

Gordon, S. (2001). *Performance-Based Contracting.* Washington, DC: International City/County Management Association.

Guo, C. (2007). When government becomes the principal philanthropist: The effects of public funding on patterns of nonprofit governance. *Public Administration Review* 67(3): 458–473.

Guo, C., and Musso, J. (2007). Representation in nonprofit and voluntary sector organizations: A conceptual framework. *Nonprofit and Voluntary Sector Quarterly* 36(2): 308–326.

Herman, R., and Renz, D. (1997). Multiple constituencies and the social construction of nonprofit organization effectiveness. *Nonprofit and Voluntary Sector Quarterly* 26(2): 185–206.

Hillman, A., Withers, M., and Collins, B. (2009). Resource dependence theory: A review. *Journal of Management* 35(6): 1404–1427.

Kapucu, N. (2006). Interagency communication networks during emergencies: Boundary spanners in multiagency coordination. *American Review of Public Administration* 36(2): 207–225.

Leardini, C., Moggi, S., and Rossi, G. (2018). The new era of stakeholder engagement: Gaining, maintaining, and repairing legitimacy in nonprofit organizations. *International Journal of Public Administration* 42(6): 520–532.

Leipnitz, S. (2014). Stakeholder performance measurement in nonprofit organizations: Case study of a donor satisfaction barometer. *Nonprofit Management and Leadership* 25(2): 165–181.

LeRoux, K. (2009). Managing stakeholder demands: Balancing responsiveness to clients and funding agents in nonprofit social organizations. *Administration & Society* 41(2): 158–184.

Lewis, D. (2001). *The Management of Non-Governmental Development Organizations: An Introduction.* New York: Routledge.

Lindblom, C. (1994). The implications of organizational legitimacy for corporate social performance and disclosure. Paper presented at the Critical Perspectives on Accounting Conference, New York.

Mara, C. (2000). A strategic planning process for a small nonprofit organization: A hospice example. *Nonprofit Management and Leadership* 11(2): 211–223.

Martin, L. (2001). *Financial Management for Human Service Administrators.* Long Grove, IL: Waveland Press.

Martin, L. (2002). Performance-based contracting for human services: Lessons for public procurement? *Journal of Public Performance* 2(1): 2002–2071

McDonald, C. (1997). Government, funded nonprofits, and accountability. *Nonprofit Management & Leadership* 8(1): 51–64.

Miller, J. (2002). The board as a monitor of organizational activity: The applicability of agency theory to nonprofit boards. *Nonprofit Management & Leadership* 12(4): 429–450.

National Council on Community Foundations. (1961). *Community Foundations in the United States and Canada 1914–1961.* Washington, DC: Council on Community Foundations.

Nelson, Aiko A., and Gazley, B. (2014). The rise of school-supporting nonprofits. *Education Finance and Policy* 9(4): 541–66.

Ospina, S., Diaz, W., and O'Sullivan, J. (2002). Negotiating accountability: Managerial lessons from identity-based nonprofit organizations. *Nonprofit and Voluntary Sector Quarterly* 31(1): 5–31.

Pestoff, V., Osborne, S., and Brandsen, T. (2006). Patterns of co-production in public services: Some concluding thoughts. *Public Management Review* 8(4): 591–95.

Pfeffer, J., and Salancik, G. (1978). *The External Control of Organizations: A Resource Dependence Perspective*. New York: Harper & Row.

Pill, M. (2019). Embedding in the city? Locating civil society in the philanthropy of place. *Community Development Journal* 54(2): 179–196.

Ranucci, R., and Lee, H. (2019). Donor influence on long-term innovation within nonprofit organizations. *Nonprofit and Voluntary Sector Quarterly* 48(5): 1045–1065.

Renz, L., Lawrence, S., and Kendzior, J. (1999). *Foundation Giving: Yearbook of Facts and Figures on Private, Corporate and Community Foundations*. New York: Foundation Center.

Saidel, J. (1991). Resource interdependence: The relationship between state agencies and nonprofit organizations. *Public Administration Review* 51(6): 543–553.

Salamon, L. (1999). The nonprofit sector at a crossroads: The case of America. *Voluntas: International Journal of Voluntary and Nonprofit Organizations* 10(1): 5–23.

Salamon, L., ed. (2002). *The Tools of Government: A Guide to the New Governance*. Oxfordshire, England: Oxford University Press.

Saxton, G., Kuo, J., and Ho, Y. (2012). The determinants of voluntary financial disclosure by non-profit organizations. *Nonprofit and Voluntary Sector Quarterly* 41(6): 1051–1071.

Saxton, G. D., Neely, D. G., and Guo, C. (2014). Web disclosure and the market for charitable contributions. *Journal of Accounting and Public Policy* 33(2): 127–144.

Schatteman, A., and Bingle, B. (2015). Philanthropy supporting government: An analysis of local library funding. *Journal of Public and Nonprofit Affairs* 1(2): 74–86.

Smith, S. R. (2010). Nonprofits and public administration: Reconciling performance measurement and citizen engagement. *American Review of Public Administration* 40(2): 129–152.

Stone, C. (2015). Reflections on regime politics: From governing coalition to urban political order. *Urban Affairs Review* 51(1): 101–137.

Sundaramurthy, C., and Lewis, M. (2003). Control and collaboration: Paradoxes of governance. *Academy of Management Review* 28(3): 397–415.

Torfing, J., Sorensen, E., and Roiseland, A. (2019). Transforming the public sector into an arena for co-creation: Barriers, drivers, benefits, and ways forward. *Administration & Society* 51(5): 795–825.

Tremblay-Boire, J., and Prakash, A. (2015). Accountability.org: Online disclosures by U.S. nonprofits. *Voluntas: International Journal of Voluntary and Nonprofit Organizations* 26(2): 693–719.

Tschirhart, M. (1996). *Artful Leadership: Managing Stakeholder Problems in Nonprofit Arts Organizations.* Bloomington, IN: Indiana University Press.

Van Puyvelde, S., Caers, R., Du Bois, C., and Jegers, M. (2012). The governance of nonprofit organizations: Integrating agency theory with stakeholder and stewardship theories. *Nonprofit and Voluntary Sector Quarterly* 41(3): 431–451.

Van Slyke, D. M. (2006). Agents or stewards: Using theory to understand the government-nonprofit social service contracting relationship. *Journal of Public Administration Research and Theory* 17: 157–187.

Van Til, J. (1994). Nonprofit organizations and social institutions. In *The Jossey-Bass Handbook of Nonprofit Leadership and Management,* 2nd ed., edited by R. D. Herman and Associates, 39–62. San Francisco: Jossey-Bass.

Willems, J., and Faulk, L. (2019). Does voluntary disclosure matter when nonprofit organizations violate stakeholder trust? *Journal of Behavioral Public Administration* 2(1): 1–16.

Witesman, E., and Fernandez, S. (2013). Government contracts with private organizations: Are there differences between nonprofits and for-profits? *Nonprofit and Voluntary Sector Quarterly* 42(4): 689–715.

Young, D., and Steinberg, R. (1995). *Economics for Nonprofit Managers.* New York: The Foundation Center.

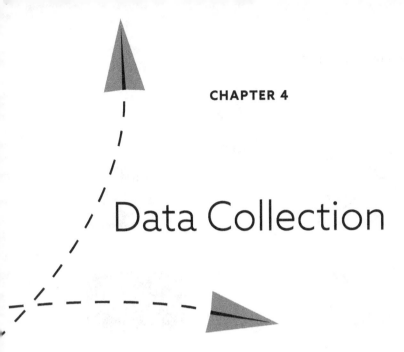

CHAPTER 4

Data Collection

KEY POINTS

1. Data consist of information collected and analyzed for the purpose of understanding where the organization has been and where it currently is in order to plan for the future.
2. Data form a critical component of any strategic planning exercise.
3. Administrative data are particularly important to the strategic planning process.
4. Primary data collection is often necessary but is also the most time-consuming data to gather.

Strategic planning begins with a solid understanding of where the organization has been and where it is now. To gain this understanding, we rely on various data-collection methods and sources, which will be explored in this chapter. Data (or broadly speaking, information) are necessary because they point out where there are any challenges not being met and where the organization is doing well. Data help the organization evaluate and prioritize competing issues

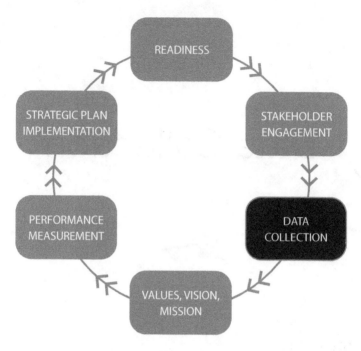

FIGURE 8
Cycle of Strategic Planning

to focus the strategic plan. The process of data collection and analysis also reinforces or begins a culture of data-driven decision-making that is needed for a successful strategic planning process and implementation (for more detail, refer to chapter 3, which discusses organizational cultures). To make strategic goals clear and measurable, the organization must know its starting point; then progress can be measured in the plan. For example, a strategic goal that simply states, "Provide quality educational experiences," is not specific or measurable. We don't know how the organization is accomplishing that goal now nor where it wants to be in the future. Data give us a baseline.

Furthermore, data collection focuses the organization on measuring the right things rather than measuring for the sake of it (MacLaughlin 2016). Funders often require information that is not used by the organization, which leads to a general apathy toward data. For example, the organization may be very interested to know how many people are served in a certain geographic region. While this number is useful, the organization may need to focus on how well those services are being delivered or the rate of completion, in addition to measuring the number of individuals served. We need to shift compliance data collection to informative data collection, which is possible if we get input from staff and form measurable goals. Similarly, the data will never tell an organization what to do or how to do it. Therefore, the organization needs to think through the desired level of performance; in essence, it should ask, "How good is good?"

Along the same lines as the book by Jim Collins, *Good to Great* (2005), we know there are hundreds of thousands of good nonprofit organizations in this country (see chapter 2). But nonprofits must decide what level of performance defines success for them. For example, an all-volunteer organization that runs a food pantry once per week may consider itself a success if its food donations for the week meet the demand for that food—no food is wasted and all the families' needs are met. Another nonprofit organization might define success a little differently and may be more focused on the long term. For example, an organization that operates a drug treatment center may consider itself a success if 60% of its clients don't return to drug treatment within two years of their initial treatment. Sometimes performance standards (how good is good) can be defined by an external partner such as a government agency or accrediting body. Other times the organization can determine its own performance expectations. In many instances, this discussion of performance does not occur at all, which leaves staff and the board struggling to create a goal-oriented strategic plan without clear direction on what good performance even is. For example, if I say I want to be a good parent, what does that mean? Is being a good parent measured by how much time I spend with my child, how many after-school activities they are involved in, how much money I spend on quality daycare, what schools they go to, how much physical activity they get, how many books I read to them? We can define being a good parent in many ways. Like a parent, an organization needs to define what "good" means to them, and then everyone in the organization needs to work together toward that larger purpose. This purpose is commonly expressed in the mission, but it may not be well understood.

> case example #5

An organization had a long history of serving the community by providing transportation, programs, and other services to seniors. The nonprofit had a diverse revenue stream and sufficient cash reserves. Staff and board leadership were stable. Overall the organization was doing well, and it was particularly efficient with resources. Some new board members, however, wanted to know how well their services were meeting the needs of seniors in their community. In essence, they were asking, "How effective is the organization?" It was an intriguing question. Some staff were offended because they thought it implied they were not doing their jobs. Some staff had wonderful stories to tell about the seniors who'd thanked them, so they thought they must be doing well. Others were not so sure. No one had directly asked the question before. How well are they doing at meeting the needs of seniors? Is meeting seniors' needs the mission of the organization? If so, to what end? Or is it the purpose of the organization to do more, to serve more? These were all intriguing questions that needed to be examined. With several new board members having just joined, the time was right to start thinking about these questions in a strategic planning process. The staff and board would be involved, but so would the seniors and their families—important stakeholders. The organization also wanted to involve some of its major funding partners, particularly county staff and elected officials. Working through the strategic planning process, they created a plan that included not only partnering with the county on a new research project to assess the quality of life of seniors in the community but also being more intentional about collecting information, qualitative and quantitative, about the seniors' experiences and their quality of life as a result of the organization's programs.

𝄇

More often than not, I have seen organizations use a formula loosely called "better than last year" without a clear sense of the desired performance. Furthermore, the board may have a different idea of success than the staff. For example, staff at an organization that provides mental-health services may be particularly interested in the long-term impact of their services on the whole family. Because of the broader implications, they may look at the household as a unit of service rather than the individual who is receiving care. Staff may ask an individual about the children in the household to determine whether they are enrolled and attending school, and whether the family has stable housing. But what is reported to a funder or possibly the board is the number of units of service and whether that service is efficiently delivered. Chapter 5 will go into detail about defining and creating performance measures. To prepare for the process, a nonprofit should begin by answering these questions:

- What do you currently do (activities, programs, services)?
- Why do you do these things?
- How do you know if you're doing them well and how do you currently measure this?
- What are your performance expectations, or how good is good?

Administrative Data

To begin the data-collection stage, I suggest looking internally first—at your organization's administrative data. I recommend a kind of data audit, where you figure out where information lives in the organization, who has it, what do they do with it, what systems are involved, and how that information is reported (or not). Organizations collect financial data (budget, bank accounts, investments, etc.). Who is responsible for those data, who has access to those data, and how are those data reported? What do your numbers tell you?

Financial Data

With the growth of the nonprofit sector and the increase in the number of courses and degree programs available in nonprofit management, research on nonprofit finances has also grown (Schatteman and Waymire 2017). We understand more about how financially healthy nonprofits are and what leads to better overall financial health. Non-profit financial capacity is defined as having sufficient resources to take advantage of opportunities as well as respond to financial threats (Bowman 2011). During challenging financial periods, nonprofits often must make some hard decisions about whether to take on debt, reduce services, or lay off staff. If organizations have sufficient cash reserves, they are better able to sustain operations during financial downturns. Having financial capacity also means nonprofit organizations can expand operations and seize opportunities. In a 2018 study, 86% of nonprofits stated demand for their services keeps rising (Nonprofit Finance Fund). Researchers have examined the importance of revenue diversification and the prevalence of operating reserves on financial stability of nonprofits (Chikoto and Neely 2014; Calabrese 2013; 2011; Blackwood and Pollak 2009, 10; Carrol and Stater 2008; Tuckman and Chang 1991). In addition to the academic study of nonprofit cash reserves, there have been recent reports of nonprofits hoarding cash. For example, Wounded Warrior Project held one year of expenses in cash, significantly more than the recommended three months (Phillips 2016). Nonprofit organizations are caught in a paradox of savings: save too little or save too much? (Booth 2012). Perhaps the most public case of spending cash versus saving cash is the American Red Cross, which has been scrutinized by the public and the media on several occasions (Elliot and Sullivan 2015). Nonprofit managers are under pressure to spend down any savings, even if the savings should be reserved for a future major financial event, such as the COVID-19 pandemic (Mitchell 2017). Lam and McDougle (2016) developed a model of six measures of financial health as conceptualized by Bowman to examine the relationships among these measures and the indicators of community vulnerability. Their results indicate that variation exists in four of the six outcome measures (equity ratio, months of spending, mark up, and months of liquidity) and that contextual effects (e.g., being located in a minority or low-mobility community) partially explain these variances (2016). It is logical that operating reserves, savings, should help an organization plan for an unpredictable future, which should promote longer-term thinking. Some researchers have termed this "fiscal slack," which allows an organization to quickly respond to changing economic conditions even though managers are pressured to spend rather than save (Mitchell 2015). Mitchell and Calabrese (2018) wrote about this and other "proverbs," which included minimizing overhead expenses, diversifying revenue, avoiding debt, and reducing surplus and reserves. Despite these pressures, it is recommended that nonprofits have a minimum of three months of cash reserves, but that is dependent on many factors such as type of nonprofit, physical infrastructure, and general economic conditions (Nonprofit Finance Fund 2018).

There are many ways to measure financial health, but I focus on five key financial ratios. I also recommend looking at these financial indicators over a five-year period, which offers a clearer picture than a one- or two-year snapshot.

1. <u>Net income</u>: revenue versus expenses annually and over the past five years. Where is the trend line?
2. <u>Fund balance</u>: total assets versus total liabilities annually and over the past five years. Are assets increasing or declining?
3. <u>Leverage ratio</u>: total debt divided by total assets over the past five years and converted to a percentage. High values indicate future liquidity problems as reduced capacity for future borrowing. The table below summarizes the results for a nonprofit that indicates their leverage ratio has been going down over the past five years. They are paying down debt and increasing assets.

Total assets	$2,208,819	$2,153,183	$2,043,435	$2,059,754	$2,192,785
Loans and notes	$494,925	$450,500	$275,437	$209,617	$190,472
Leverage ratio	22.41%	20.92%	13.48 %	10.18%	8.69%

FIGURE 9
Leverage Ratio

4. <u>Revenue mix</u>: expressed as a percentage of total revenue and over the past five years. Concentration of revenue sources could lead to instability if there is a sharp decline in any one area, particularly related to grants. It's okay to have higher percentages for individual contributions, which tend to be more stable than external sources where funding priorities can shift.

The following figure is an example of an organization's revenue mix expressed as a pie chart for a board summary report. The board can quickly see where most of the revenue is coming from and where the potential for growth likely lies.

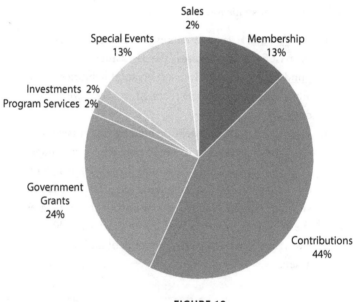

FIGURE 10
Revenue Mix

You can also express revenue as a bar chart and then indicate a trend line. See this example.

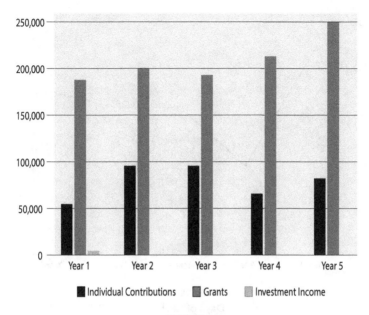

FIGURE 11
Revenue Sources

5. <u>Liquidity ratio</u>: cash and liquid assets divided by total expenses over the past five years to determine how many days or months of cash are on hand to cover expenses in the event of a financial shock. As mentioned earlier, the recommended minimum is three months of cash.

TABLE 2. CALCULATION OF DAYS OF CASH OVER FIVE-YEAR PERIOD

	Year 1	Year 2	Year 3	Year 4	Year 5
Total expenses	$263,549	$348,331	$291,396	$303,844	$333,588
Cash and equivalent	$193,080	$141,002	$166,616	$173,554	$205,353
Days of cash	267.4	147.8	208.7	208.5	224.7

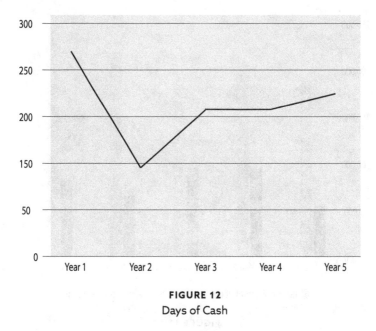

FIGURE 12
Days of Cash

The graph above indicates that this nonprofit's liquidity declined substantially in year 2 but then improved in the following three years. The organization has about 200 days of cash on hand, well beyond the minimum of three months and the desired six months.

Once these five financial ratios are determined, the organization will know exactly what its financial health looks like. These ratios will also help an organization prioritize financial health over other issues. You might find these graphics useful in discussions about your own revenue streams, for example at a strategic planning board retreat.

You will notice I did not include an analysis of organizational expenses categories (administration or management, fundraising, and program) from the IRS 990 form. In the late 1980s and early 1990s there was a movement to increase accountability in nonprofit organizations. What resulted were changes to the IRS 990 form and the inclusion of a section on the form for nonprofits to allocate their expenses into three categories—administration, program, and fundraising—with pressure to show program expenses as high as possible, which resulted in a program expense ratio (program expenses divided by total expenses). The three big charity watchdog organizations (Charity Navigator, GuideStar, and Better Business Bureau) all created arbitrary program ratios and included this ratio in their ratings of nonprofits. What happened was completely predictable: nonprofit organizations began reporting higher program ratios and reducing investment in administration, and not just in salaries but in things like technology, accounting, professional development, and so on. There is no evidence that shows what percentage of administrative cost leads to better program outcomes. Nor is there any clear research taking place in a nonprofit that would allow it to accurately track every hour spent during the day so staff hours could be allocated across these expense categories. Left with a void of actual data on program and organizational performance (see chapter 6), however, the public is left with this inaccurate and misleading measure called "the program ratio." I do not support its use because of the bad data-collection methods and the arbitrary nature of the definitions upon which the ratio is based. This measure has had many unintended consequences in addition to the ones mentioned above, such as nonprofit organizations reducing or eliminating indirect cost rates on contracts, thereby reducing their internal capacity to provide services. For more information about this phenomenon, now referred to as the "overhead myth," check out some of these resources: Charity Navigator 2014; Berger, Harold, and Taylor 2013; Pallotta 2013.

Program Data

A second large area of administrative data is program data. This information comes from the programs and services offered by the organization to its clients or users. You'll want to gather data related to such things as the number of hours open to the public or the number of people served, as well as staff size relative to client population, among other program indicators. Here is an example of program data covering several years.

This is also a time to determine how program data are collected, by whom, and whether the data are shared or used by staff in their

TABLE 3. EXAMPLE OF MEASURING PROGRAM
PARTICIPATION

	Number of adult programs	Adult program attendance	Number of child programs	Child program attendance
2019	117	1,137	274	6,803
2018	90	1,795	337	7,408
2017	139	2,646	399	7,289
2016	92	3,334	462	7,833
2015	77	12,509	595	12,515
2014	47	21,449	682	10,775
2013	369	2,039	835	15,886

day-to-day decision-making. An organization may want to consider what program questions they have but can't answer with their current data-collection methods and processes. This could be an issue that the strategic plan could address. Overall the organization wants to understand who they serve and how. Program-level data are often reported as an aggregate in quarterly or annual reports to funders or other outside entities. The purpose of this exercise in assessing what program data you already have is to hopefully inform any changes in your future data collection.

➤ case example #6

Most nonprofit organizations don't have data analysts on staff, nor can they afford to contract that work out. Typically data collection and analysis are part of the administrative responsibilities of the executive director or other senior staff. In this case, a funder was asking for program data for a specific program they funded—a reasonable request, except that this funder only funded 10% of the program but wanted 100% of all data about that program. During a strategic planning exercise, this concern was brought up by staff as they talked about the burden of data collection. As part of the planning process, the consultant reached out to the funder to talk about their grant requirements and the reporting burden for such a small amount of funding. After some senior staff were brought into the conversation, the grant funder agreed to ask only for program data related to the portion of participants they funded. The funder had been unaware of the cost of data collection and analysis, in terms of staff time, but the strategic planning process resolved this issue—one the organization didn't think could be resolved. In the end, the strategic plan did include putting additional resources in future budgets toward data collection and analysis, and reporting on those results more consistently.

Λ

Human Resource Data

Another area often overlooked in the data-collection process is related to human-resource data. Personnel is the single largest expense in any nonprofit because nearly all nonprofits provide services that require human resources, whether paid or unpaid. Administrative data for human resources may include the size of payroll; type of staff responsibilities; demographic characteristics of the workforce; educational levels of employees; number of work hours provided each day, week, month, or quarter; employee attrition; years of service; employee retirement eligibility; workplace safety issues; and more. Many nonprofits rely on volunteer labor and often track the number of volunteers annually; number of volunteer hours provided each day, week, month, or quarter; volunteer attrition; years of service; demographic characteristics of volunteers; and so on.

➤ case example #7

Through the strategic planning process, the board of a nonprofit museum wanted to better understand their personnel costs relative to similar organizations in their region. This was important information as they wanted to make sure their senior staff was being adequately compensated. The organization had some turnover in senior staff a few years earlier, and they knew how

TABLE 4. EXAMPLE OF EXECUTIVE DIRECTOR SALARY COMPARISON

Organization	Number of staff	Executive director's salary	Executive director's salary as % of total expenses	Total salaries	Total salaries as % of total expenses
St. Charles	4	$36,615	24.87%	$61,419	41.72%
Des Plaines	4	$47,658	24.88%	$140,156	73.16%
Elgin	5	$48,744	24.15%	$74,519	36.92%
Geneva	6	$50,150	15.64%	$160,049	49.91%
Glen Ellyn	7	$44,135	23.52%	$87,160	46.44%
Lombard	8	$57,115	33.54%	$103,028	60.50%

disruptive that was, especially to a small organization. As part of the data-collection process, they wanted to understand the market rate of their executive director's salary in relation to overall salaries and total expenses for the organization. The consultant created the following table to compare history museums in select Illinois cities based on the number of staff, the salary of the executive director (and as a percentage of total expenses), the total cost of salaries, and total salaries as a percentage of total expenses. With this information, the board could determine whether one of their goals should be to increase the executive director's salary over time.

There are several places where an organization can learn more about nonprofit salaries. A good place to start is the salary information listed on the organization's IRS 990 form, which is publicly available on GuideStar (Candid 2022). You can also purchase salary surveys such as GuideStar's *Nonprofit Compensation Report*. The most recent report costs $399 for a single user and $999 for multi-user access (2021). You should also check with your state nonprofit association and any professional trade associations for compensation studies they might have.

Secondary Data

There may be cases in which you want to gather secondary data; that is, data that are publicly available. Examples include census data, market surveys, and salary surveys. Secondary data are useful for comparison purposes, such as population or demographic changes over time. These data can inform decisions about program offerings or future demand. The challenges with secondary data include limited access and the inability to manipulate the data. Often this type of information appears in a summary report, and the information can't be manipulated for particular circumstances. Here is an example of a table produced by Data USA using the *American Community Survey*. Data USA allows users to customize publicly available data (Deloitte and Datawheel n.d.).

You can also try the On the Map application by the US Census Bureau (2017). This tool is useful when analyzing geographic data, and it allows you to export the data into shapefiles for geographical information system (GIS) analysis. I used this app to analyze the inflow and outflow of workers in a geographical area (see figure below). I was then able to determine how many individuals lived and worked in St. Charles compared to how many workers commuted into St. Charles but lived outside it, as well as how many St. Charles

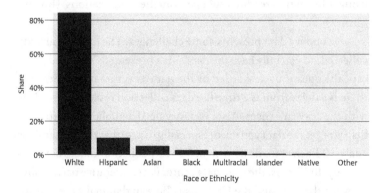

FIGURE 13
Race and Ethnicity in St. Charles, IL
Table created using 2020 data from the US Census Bureau

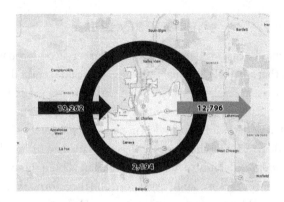

FIGURE 14
Inflow vs. Outflow of Population

residents commuted outside the city for work. These numbers were valuable when thinking about volunteer recruitment.

Other types of secondary data include website analysis, printed reports or documents, calendars of events, books, media stories, committee minutes, and other materials that help an organization understand what has been written about it and understand the geographic and political context the organization is in. You might find it useful to compare your organization with others in a similar area. The following table compares revenue for nonprofit theatres in Illinois using information readily available from the organizations' IRS 990 forms.

Secondary data presents some challenges. The data are already collected, so you only have the data as it's presented. You need to accept the questions as worded or the data as summarized. Second, there is a delay from the time the data collection took place, such as with the 10-year census. Also, you may need a public data expert to help you get the data you need, especially in a format that's useful for analysis. Each state deals with access to publicly available data differently. In Illinois, the state data center is a cooperative partnership between the state and the US Census Bureau that makes census information available to the public through a network of organizations. This decentralized approach means there are two organizations in

TABLE 5. THEATRE COMPARISONS

Revenue	Egyptian Theatre, DeKalb		Genesee Theatre, Waukegan		Paramount Theatre, Aurora	
	%	2015	%	2015	%	2015
Contributions	8.58%	$25,641	43.86%	$2,119,438	90.87%	$1,191,465
Government grants		$0		$0	4.85%	$63,612
Program services	84.73%	$253,144	55.70%	$2,691,530		$0
Investments	0.01%	$15		$5		$25
Special events		$0		$0	4.28%	$56,108
Sales	6.69%	$19,983		$0		$0
Other		$0	0.44%	$21,321		$0
Total revenue		$298,783		$4,832,294		$1,311,210

Illinois that act as coordinating agencies for the state, which are the Chicago Metropolitan Agency for Planning and the Center for Governmental Studies at Northern Illinois University (n.d.). If, after all this work gathering data, you still need information about your programs, services, personnel, volunteers, staff, community, or funders that you can't find in administrative or secondary data, then you must do your own primary data collection.

Primary Data

Primary data collection refers to the process of collecting information specifically for your strategic planning process. It is the most expensive and the most time-consuming kind of data collection, which is why you should try to use administrative and secondary data first. Designing any research may also require assistance from outside your organization if you do not have the necessary time or skills within it. The goal of primary data collection is to generate enough input as efficiently as possible so the strategic planning process can adhere to the planning schedule. There are several methods of primary data collection to consider, and I'll outline each.

Online Surveys

One of the most efficient ways to gather information is to use an online survey. This option was particularly valuable while COVID-19 pandemic restrictions were in place, but online surveys are always useful to reduce the time and effort needed from staff and to offer all stakeholders an equal opportunity to participate. For mail surveys, high response rates are considered to be from 20% to 30% (Hager et al. 2003). Although mail surveys may achieve a higher response rate, online surveys show no difference in the respondents' characteristics such as demographics (Lin and Van Ryzin 2012). You do, however, want to consider distributing paper copies of the survey if your stakeholder population might be unlikely to participate in an online survey; meaning, individuals with limited access to the Internet or little technology experience. You can also add some incentives for participating, such as raffling guest passes, gift cards, or free memberships depending on your organization. There are many platforms to choose from to conduct an online survey, including SurveyMonkey, Qualtrics, and Google Forms. The following questions should be customized based on the stakeholder analysis you've conducted and the mission of your organization.

SURVEY QUESTIONS

1. Indicate your current relationship to the organization. Check all that apply.
   a. Board member
   b. Donor
   c. Service recipient, user, member, etc.
   d. Volunteer
   e. Staff
   f. Community member
   g. Schoolteacher

    h. Local business owner

    i. Elected official

    j. Government employee

    k. Foundation

    l. Other: _____

2. Where do you live? (Include zip code, county, city, etc.)

    _____

3. Indicate how often you use or visit the following to learn about this organization.

    a. Organization's social media accounts

    b. Organization's website

    c. Local news

    d. Word of mouth

    e. Other: _____

4. What do you love most about this organization? _____

    _____

5. What do you feel are the biggest challenges for this organization? _____

    _____

6. What are two or three things this organization should focus on in the next three years and why? _____

    _____

7. Do you have any additional comments or suggestions you'd like to make?_____

    _____

8. If you're interested in speaking with us directly, please leave your contact information here: _____

    _____

Organizations should solicit responses to the online survey through a variety of mechanisms, including a membership newsletter, social media, press releases, postcards, and email announcements.

In terms of summarizing the results, I recommend creating tables or charts that are visually interesting. These can be put in a written report or shared in a presentation to the board to engage members with results. Take a look at these examples.

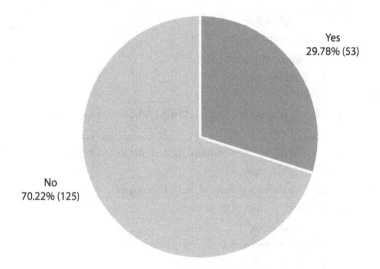

FIGURE 15
Example of a Pie Chart

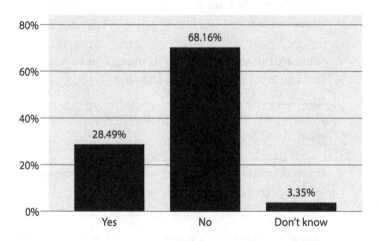

FIGURE 16
Example of a Bar Chart

Answers to open-ended survey questions should be summarized in themes. A word cloud is sometimes useful for visually demonstrating themes, such as the example below. Word clouds can be created in online survey platforms (including SurveyMonkey and Qualtrics).

Small Exposure Making Generation Exhibits Volunteer Keep Available Staff
Think **Museum** St. Charles **Space** Displays **Funding**
Interest **People** Needs **Community** Visit **History** Raising
Relevant Probably Money Visitors New Awareness Know

FIGURE 17
Example of a Word Cloud

I'd like to caution organizations about collecting only survey data—there are some negative aspects to this method. Public surveys tend to have very low response rates. The closer a person is to the organization, the more likely they are to take time to complete a survey. So volunteers are very likely, but the average member of the public is least likely. In addition, if an organization wants to understand why an individual thinks or acts a certain way, this information is likely best gathered through a qualitative approach with open-ended questions. Surveys tend to work best for short, multiple-choice questions. Keep in mind, they are most efficient at getting responses to questions dealing with "what is happening" or "how frequently." Also, the people who complete surveys may not be as thoughtful as you'd like; they might rush through questions or complete them incorrectly, making the data unreliable.

➤ case example #8

During the data-collection phase of strategic planning, the executive director expressed that their accrediting agency wanted the organization to survey current program participants about their experiences with the organization's services and that the same survey could inform the strategic planning process. The survey the nonprofit created had a total of 62 questions, mainly of the Likert-scale type ("On a scale of 1–5 how would you rate the following programs?"), for over 50 programs. Staff sent the survey out in an email and made paper copies available in the lobby. Participants returned 12 paper copies. After several reminders from program staff, the organization received 124 responses to the survey. The board was happy with the response rate, despite it being just 4% of participants in all programs. Staff summarized the survey results and presented them to the strategic planning committee. Over-whelmingly, all programs received high scores. There seemed to be little room for improvement, at least according to this survey. The consultant noted there were several flaws in the survey that the organization should consider. First, the survey was developed by their accrediting body without any customization based on the actual programs delivered by this organization. For example, 89% of participants gave the pool a high satisfaction score, but the organization didn't have a pool on-site. In fact, survey respondents rated all programs very highly. Second, there were no qualifying questions before the satisfaction questions; so everyone rated every program even if they hadn't participated in all of them. Once the consultant pointed out these survey flaws and skewed results, the group decided to use other types of data to inform the strategic planning process.

⋀

Focus Groups

While online surveys may be an efficient way to gather information from a broad array of people, sometimes speaking directly with individuals is helpful to truly understand their perspectives. This may take the form of focus groups and interviews. First we'll look at focus groups. In general, focus groups are useful when speaking to a sub-set of people about issues they're comfortable discussing in front of others, especially their peers. For example, holding a focus group of volunteers to gather information about the volunteer orientation pro-gram would be very effective. People feel more comfortable sharing their perspectives with others they have already built relationships with and the topic is not very sensitive. If necessary, Focus groups can effectively be done virtually too. The size of the group depends on the facilitation skills of the person leading it, whether the session will be recorded or notes will be taken, and whether there is a dedicated notetaker if needed. In general, focus groups for nonprofit organizations work well with five to eight people involved (Krueger and Casey 2009).

In terms of recruitment for the focus group, the nonprofit should decide on a strategy. If a cross section of community members is desired, then a broader recruitment strategy is appropriate using social media. For example, St. Charles History Museum, an organization I worked with on their strategic plan, created a number of strategies to recruit community members, including a press release to local media, newsletter announcements, and social media posts. See the following example of a Facebook post used for this purpose.

St. Charles History Museum
April 5, 2019 · 🌐

Have an idea for the Museum's future and our mission? Reminder that we are still in need of participants for Sunday's focus group at the Museum! Register at the link below.

STCMUSEUM.ORG
History Museum Focus Group
Members of the St. Charles community are invited to attend a fo...

FIGURE 18
Facebook Post to Advertise Focus Group
Courtesy of the St. Charles History Museum

The nonprofit organization may want to include a focus group with children. If so, parents or guardians should receive the questions in advance and sign a form to grant their permission to interview their child. The challenges in conducting focus groups with children are asking age-appropriate questions and encouraging participants to speak openly in front of their peers (Krueger and Casey 2009). Alternatively, you could have a focus group with the parents instead of the children.

To prepare for the focus group, the questions should be written in advance and can be shared with participants as well. The focus group should be scheduled at a time and place convenient for the participants. The only caution with focus groups is to make sure there is already a high level of trust among the participants. This will ensure an open dialogue. If you're doing a focus group of staff, I suggest separating staff members from their supervisors. A focus group needs a skilled facilitator to manage it, so I recommend that anyone thinking of leading a focus group should learn and practice appreciative inquiry techniques (Barrett and Fry 2005; Cooperrider and Srivastva 1987). Appreciative inquiry is a theory and methodological approach that encourages participants to come to a shared vision of the future based on their values. It can be a useful methodology for a strategic planning process and involves a four-stage cycle of discovery, dream, design, and destiny—all linked to the central focus of a future vision. Appreciative inquiry has been used to cocreate visions with large groups as well, called AI summits (Barrett and Fry 2005).

To be effective, a focus group needs to be guided by good questions. For a strategic planning session, I typically start with broad questions, leaving room to spark further discussion but providing enough structure to focus the conversation. Comments from participants help others make connections as well. The role of the facilitator is to manage the conversation and make sure all participants have an opportunity to share their perspectives. I also like to start with easier questions to get the conservation going and then move to more focused questions as the conversation progresses. Good focus-group questions, according to Krueger and Casey (2009), spark good conversation, avoid jargon, are clear and simple, are short, are usually open-ended, focus on one idea at a time, and have clear directions.

Questions for strategic planning focus groups typically include the following.

- Tell us your name and describe your role with the organization.
- How long have you been associated with the organization?
- In your own words, what is the mission of the organization?
- What work by the organization are you most proud of?
- What challenges do you think the organization is facing or will likely face in the coming months or years?
- Is there anything you wish to share about this strategic planning process?

These questions can be customized further depending on the particular stakeholder group involved. For example, I always like to ask board members why they serve on the board.

Invitations for the focus group are usually best issued by the nonprofit organization. The facilitator should make sure that the nonprofit invites a diverse group of participants to ensure representation across the stakeholders. Once the focus group is arranged, the consultant or the planning committee should confirm all details, including date, time, place, parking, transportation, and any other pertinent information for participants. Reminders should be sent a week before and then a day before.

➤ case example #9

While you do want to hear a range of perspectives, and focus groups are an excellent way to capture qualitative data, you must be careful about how these groups are put together. For one organization, I divided the focus groups into various stakeholder groups. One of the larger groups was made up of staff. The executive director invited senior staff and their managers to attend a focus group. A total of 12 participants signed up, which is a little large for a focus group, but I had a helper who assisted with taking notes. I began the meeting by welcoming everyone and then posed some easier, open-ended questions. I asked everyone to introduce themselves and tell us about their role in the organization. The next round of questions involved more in-depth discussion of programs and thoughts on program areas to expand. During the discussion, it was clear that only senior leaders were responding to these questions. When managers were asked a question, they would glance around at the supervisors in the room and offer only surface-level responses. In effect, their voices were being stifled simply by being in the room with their direct supervisors. From then on, whenever I did these initial focus groups, I kept peer groups together in the first round. Later I could mix the focus groups when I felt that everyone had the freedom to offer their own opinions without the potential for censorship because of perceived or actual power differences in the room.

Before the focus-group session begins, the moderator should make sure everyone feels comfortable in the surroundings, take care of any housekeeping announcements, offer refreshments, and genuinely be appreciative of the participants' time and effort. The moderator should welcome the group and explain the purpose as well as the ground rules for the session. This person should explain how the focus group will be conducted and how information will be captured, such as whether there will be a notetaker or a recording of the conversation in audio or video format. The moderator should explain that all comments will be kept confidential and no names of persons or organizations will be used in any summary documents. Participants should be reminded that their participation is completely voluntary and that they can choose not to participate at any time.

Occasionally focus groups don't go according to plan. Even if reminded, participants may choose at the last minute not to attend. Sometimes participants will show up but with additional people who were not signed up, and the moderator has to decide what to do or say in that moment. Parents may decide to bring their children to focus groups. If the conversation is not inappropriate for children, then there typically is no reason not to proceed—but be prepared to pause the discussion just in case. Some participants may not readily contribute in an open conversation, so the moderator will have to use a different approach, such as breaking into smaller groups (if there are additional notetakers available or some way to capture ideas on paper) or going to each person for their responses. One of the challenges of moderating is to make sure the participants have enough time to respond to the questions while also keeping the session within the allotted time. Keeping to a schedule is an important show of respect for everyone's time.

At the end of the session, the moderator should summarize the main points of the discussion and ask the group whether this summary reflects what they heard. If there is time, the moderator can ask whether there is anything missing from the summary. Before ending the meeting, the moderator should thank the participants. The consultant or planning committee should follow up with a thank-you to all participants and let them know about next steps in the process.

In terms of data analysis, the strategic planning consultant or the person responsible for the process would then summarize the responses for each of the focus-group questions and determine if any particular themes developed. The organization may want to select certain statements (without name attribution) to share in the summary report. The quotations provide evidence of the conservation in the words of the participants.

There are criticisms of the focus-group method of data collection. Like many other methods, focus groups rely on a person's memory about their thoughts or behaviors. In addition, while they're effective for gathering information about a person's perceptions, they may not be effective if you're discussing sensitive information that a participant wouldn't want to share publicly or with their peers. To encourage in-depth discussions, you can adjust the focus-group size, giving adequate time for each participant to make meaningful contributions. Dominant individuals can try to take over the group, which is why a skilled moderator is needed. Keep in mind, you can learn a great deal about people and their attitudes simply by observing behavior in a focus group.

➤ case example #10

Encouraging the expression of diverse opinions in a focus group can really help when you want to evaluate all possibilities and shine a light on issues not easily detected. When moderating a focus group in a low-income neighborhood, we brought together community leaders, neighborhood activists, elected officials, and program participants. We did this to ensure all the voices in that neighborhood were well represented. When well-intentioned individuals go into a community seeking opinions, they are often not trusted because the community may have a history of "being studied" but then seeing no change to their circumstances as a result. Community members justifiably become disillusioned and disheartened by these processes. Sincere efforts should be made to include them though; invite them into the conversations in whatever way they want to participate, while respecting their lived experiences and contributions. This necessity was never more apparent to me than when I was facilitating a community focus group. We were very excited that at least four community members trusted us enough to share their ideas and concerns. The focus group was set up to gather information about job opportunities in the community. While there were job openings that matched the backgrounds and skills of people in the neighborhood, the jobs were going unfilled and community leaders wanted to know why. After some time discussing this, community members shared with the larger group that many of the residents did not own their own vehicle and relied on public transportation to get to and from work. The advertised jobs offering the highest pay were not on a bus route. Other jobs were difficult to get to by bus, requiring transfers to get there. The other participants in the room had been looking at the problem through their own lenses—not from the residents' perspective—since they did not take the bus to and from work. We thought we had identified the problem before the session, but the focus group revealed the real issue.

人

Interviews

Interviews are particularly effective with individuals who don't wish to share information publicly, such as donors, funders, former volunteers, and elected officials. Organizations can use in-depth interviews to "explore in detail the experiences, motives, and opinions of others and learn to see the world from perspectives other than their own" (Rubin and Rubin 2012, 3).

Interviews can be done in person or virtually. Most importantly, they should be scheduled at a convenient time and place for the person being interviewed. There are three types of interview questions: main questions, probing questions, and follow-up questions (2012). Main questions cover the main areas the interviewer wants to capture. These questions can be given to the person in advance of being interviewed so they can think about their responses. Probing questions are used to encourage the interviewee to provide more details or examples. Follow-up questions encourage the interviewee to elaborate on their answers, which provides a more in-depth response. Overall, interviewers must be good listeners and be genuinely interested in the interviewees' thoughts.

The keys to a good interview are honesty and respect, which build trust. Most questions related to strategic planning are not likely to be sensitive, but sometimes they might be, especially if they relate to personnel or client services. The main questions can certainly be the same as the questions used in a focus group. They are good starting points and ensure that the same type of information is gathered from different groups. Before the session, the interviewer should explain how notes or recording will be done and then get permission to audio or video record the session if necessary.

In terms of analysis, the same suggestions apply as those for focus groups. The interviewee should be asked whether their responses can be attributed to them for the purposes of reporting to the board or whether they prefer to remain anonymous. Ideally, the interviewer transcribes the conversations and shares the transcript with the interviewee for review, revision, and comment, as recommended by qualitative researchers (Marshall and Rossman 2011). This will ensure that the conversation was captured correctly and there are no misunderstandings in meaning or word choice.

In summary, focus groups and interviews take a considerable amount of time to organize, conduct, and analyze. Their use will depend on the level of participation you seek from your organization's stakeholders. In both cases, you need to be clear with participants about whether their comments will remain anonymous in any reports or further discussions. Your focus groups and interviews may concentrate on the same broad issues as an online survey (strengths and weaknesses of the organization), but these conversations often lead to deeper discussions. For example, several individuals might remark that they didn't always know what events for volunteers were taking place at the organization. A skilled facilitator will ask follow-up questions about the organization's communications or outreach effort. Then, after the session, the person taking notes and doing the analysis will need to look for overall themes such as these.

Data-Collection Report

Once all the necessary information has been collected, I suggest writing a summary report for the board or the strategic planning committee. This report summarizes the results of all the data-collection efforts. It also provides the basis for the board retreat. Likely, certain issues will have surfaced from the various groups that participated. There may be agreement on these issues or disagreement, and those are good points to discuss at a board retreat. What the data-collection report should do is give the organization a baseline understanding of where they are and some ideas about where to go in the future. The strategic plan will be the road map to get there.

DISCUSSION QUESTIONS

1. If an organization does not have anyone on staff dedicated to data collection and analysis, what are other options for collecting and analyzing data?

2. What are the benefits and challenges of an online survey versus a focus group for gathering information for your strategic plan?

3. What data does your organization not currently have but you wish you had that could better inform your strategic planning process?

REFERENCES

Barrett, F., and Fry, R. (2005). *Appreciative Inquiry: A Positive Approach to Building Cooperative Capacity*. Chagrin Falls, OH: The Taos Institute.

Berger, K., Harold, J., and Taylor, A. (2013). The overhead myth. *Nonprofit Quarterly*. June 17, 2013. https://nonprofitquarterly.org/the-overhead -myth/.

Blackwood, A., and Pollak, T. (2009). *Washington-Area Nonprofit Operating Reserves*. Washington, DC: Urban Institute, Center on Nonprofits and Philanthropy.

Booth, M. (2012). In the band or on the ground: An examination of financial reserves in Australian aid organizations. Master's thesis, Queensland University of Technology. Australian Centre for Philanthropy and Nonprofit Studies.

Bowman, W. (2011). *Finance Fundamentals for Nonprofits: Building Capacity and Sustainability*. Hoboken, NJ: Wiley.

Calabrese, T. (2011). Do donors penalize nonprofit organizations with accumulated wealth? *Public Administration Review* 71: 859–869.

Calabrese, T. (2013). Running on empty: The operating reserves of US nonprofit organizations. *Nonprofit Management and Leadership* 23: 281–302.

Candid. (2021). Providing you with the nonprofit information you need. GuideStar and IRS 990 forms for donors, grantmakers, and businesses. https://www.guidestar.org.

Candid. (2022). *2022 Nonprofit Compensation Report*. GuideStar. https:// www.guidestar.org/nonprofit-compensation-report/?_gl=1*13ilkx* _ga*MTUxMTYwOTE3Ny4xNjMzMzA3MTA4*_ga_5W8PXYYGBX* MTY4MDM5NTkyNS4xMDQuMS4xNjgwMzk2MDQ1LjQ3Lj AuMA..&_ga=2.89610398.401245386.1680395926-1511609177 .1633307108.

Carroll, D., and Stater, K. (2008). Revenue diversification in nonprofit organizations: Does it lead to financial stability? *Journal of Public Administration Research and Theory* 19: 947–966.

Chikoto, G., and Neely, D. (2014). Building nonprofit financial capacity: The impact of revenue concentration and overhead costs. *Nonprofit and Voluntary Sector Quarterly* 43: 570–588.

Cooperrider, D., and Srivastva, S. (1987). Appreciative inquiry in organizational life. *Research in Organizational Change and Development* 1: 129–169.

Deloitte and Datawheel. (n.d.). Data USA: Explore, map, compare, and download US data. Data USA. https://datausa.io/.

Elliot, J., and Sullivan, L. (2015). How the Red Cross raised half a billion dollars for Haiti and built six homes. National Public Radio. https://www.propublica.org/article/how-the-red-cross-raised-half-a-billion-dollars-for-haiti-and-built-6-homes.

Hager, M., Wilson, S., Pollak, T., and Rooney, P. (2003). Response rates for mail surveys of nonprofit organizations: A review and empirical test. *Nonprofit and Voluntary Sector Quarterly* 32(2): 252–267.

Krueger, R., and Casey, M. (2009). *Focus Groups: A Practical Guide for Applied Research*. 4th ed. Thousand Oaks, CA: Sage.

Lam, M., and McDougle, L. (2016). Community variation in the financial health of nonprofit human service organizations: An examination of organizational and contextual effects. *Nonprofit and Voluntary Sector Quarterly* 45(3): 500–525.

Lin, W., and Van Ryzin, G. (2012). Web and mail surveys: An experimental comparison of methods for nonprofit research. *Nonprofit and Voluntary Sector Quarterly* 41(6): 1014–1028.

MacLaughlin, S. (2016). *Data Driven Nonprofits*. Glasgow, UK: Saltire Press.

Marshall, C., and Rossman, G. (2011). *Designing Qualitative Research*. 5th ed. Thousand Oaks, CA: Sage.

Mitchell, G. (2015). The attributes of effective NGOs and the leadership values associated with a reputation for organizational effectiveness. *Nonprofit Management and Leadership* 26(1): 39–57.

Mitchell, G. (2017). Fiscal leanness and fiscal responsiveness: Exploring the normative limits of strategic nonprofit financial management. *Administration & Society* 49(9): 1272–1296.

Mitchell, G., and Calabrese, T. (2018). Proverbs of nonprofit financial management. *American Review of Public Administration* 49(6): 649–661.

Nonprofit Finance Fund. (2018). *State of the Nonprofit Sector Survey.* https:// nff.org/learn/survey.

Pallotta, D. (2013). The way we think about charity is dead wrong. Video. TED Conferences. https://www.ted.com/talks/dan_pallotta_the_way _we_think_about_charity_is_dead_wrong.

Philipps, D. (2016). Wounded Warrior Project spends lavishly on itself, insiders say. *New York Times.* January 27, 2016.

Rubin, A., and Rubin, I. (2012). *Qualitative Interviewing: The Art of Hearing Data.* 3rd ed. Thousand Oaks, CA: Sage.

Schatteman, A., and Waymire, T. (2017). The state of nonprofit finance across disciplines. *Nonprofit Management and Leadership* 28(1): 125–137.

Torrance, H. (2012). Triangulation, respondent validation, and democratic participation in mixed methods research. *Journal of Mixed Methods Research* 6(2): 111–123.

Tuckman, H., and Chang, C. (1991). A methodology for measuring the financial vulnerability of charitable nonprofit organizations. *Nonprofit and Voluntary Sector Quarterly* 20: 445–460.

United States Census Bureau. (2017). On the map. US Census Bureau, Center for Economic Studies. https://onthemap.ces.census.gov/.

White, J. (n.d.). Illinois state data center program. Office of the Illinois Secretary of State. Accessed February 20, 2022. https://www .cyberdriveillinois.com/departments/library/depository_programs /ilsdc.html.

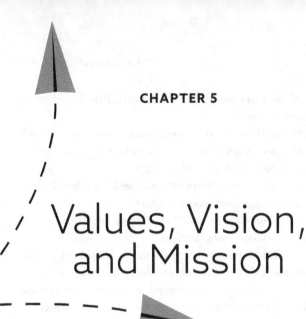

CHAPTER 5

Values, Vision, and Mission

KEY POINTS

1. The board is responsible for holding the mission in public trust.
2. For strategic planning to be successful, the organization's values, vision, and mission should align.
3. Strategic planning is an opportunity to ensure the values, vision, and mission are still relevant.

As discussed in chapter 2, the board is responsible for determining and managing the organization's values, vision, and mission. Their attachment to the organization's values positively influences the organization's performance (Cheverton 2007). Because nonprofit organizations are not owned, but rather held in public trust, the boards have a responsibility not only to the people they serve and their communities but to the broader citizenry as well. When nonprofit organizations are first formed, the founders see a need that a new nonprofit could meet. This becomes the mission. A nonprofit's mission is ever evolving, changing over time to respond to community needs and organizational maturity. While a mission is needed and is

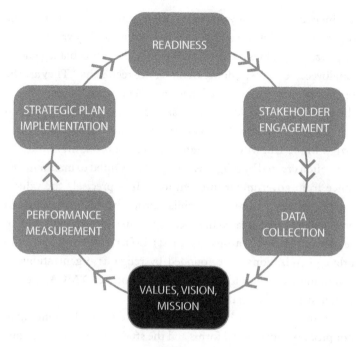

FIGURE 19
Cycle of Strategic Planning

even legally and procedurally required to create the nonprofit itself, the values and vision of the organization are the concepts that the organization must orient itself around. They form the foundation for the mission and are critical parts of the strategic planning process.

Values

Values support the work of the nonprofit, acting as the foundation. They are "management and governance tools that help test mission and determine vision and program; serve as a screen to determine the worthiness, appropriateness, and robustness of all operations; provide the framework for policies and procedures, program delivery system, communications, and fund development strategies; and evaluate whether new people align[ed] with organizational values are invited to join" (Joyaux 2015). Values can and should sync the organization's culture and behavior, creating a truly values-based organization. Values are not simply words; they unite management, employees, volunteers, donors, and service recipients. "They are the organizational expression of their members' ethical stance toward the world" (Rothschild and Milofsky 2006, 137). Values shape and are shaped by nonprofit organizations (Chen, Lune, and Quen 2013). In the US, without a state church, nonprofit organizations were often created by religious groups that wanted to maintain distance from government intervention. "It is precisely the values-expressive nature of religious, philanthropic work and the agencies engaged in it, that created the social space in which an independent sector could form" (Jeavons 1992, 404). In fact, many of today's nonprofit organizations were founded by religious organizations or communities, including Habitat for Humanity, the YMCA, the Salvation Army, and Feed the Children.

Some researchers have brought forward the understanding of nonprofit organizational forms and the study of social movements, suggesting organizational values shape society at large (Jeavons 1992). Other researchers have shown that organizations should emphasize their values to differentiate themselves, especially in the government-contracting market in which human-service organizations find themselves (Frumkin and Andre-Clark 2000). "The expressive character of nonprofit activity—the way nonprofits allow people to demonstrate commitment to social ends and values—is what significantly differentiates one nonprofit from another and what separates the nonprofit sector from other social sectors" (2000, 142). This emphasis on operational efficiency to function in a more businesslike way negates the important work that nonprofit organizations do to uphold civic and democratic societal values. Operating like a business has also led to the misguided focus on low administrative cost ratios, arbitrarily set and then publicly accepted, as an easy way to measure effectiveness and efficiency. Low cost ratios are not proxies for nonprofit efficiency or effectiveness. But nonprofit organizations experience increasing pressure to measure and justify their entire operation while being limited by program funding. See chapter 6 for more clarity about the use of performance measurement. Peter Drucker suggests that there are clear distinctions between the three sectors: "business supplies, either goods or services, government controls," but nonprofits are "human-change agents" (1990, xiv).

Rather than competing on pure efficiency measures, nonprofits should use their values and missions to differentiate themselves in the marketplace. "Nonprofits must avoid ever obscuring these differences" (Frumkin and Andre-Clark 2000, 158). Doing this, however, requires having a solid understanding of what the values of the organization actually are, building a common understanding of those values inside and outside the organization, professing those values as differentiators, and then using them in decision-making. Okun would have described this as a big trade-off between equality and equity, the core values of public service organizations, and efficiency, a core value of business (Svara and Brunet 2020; 2005; Woolridge 1998; Frederickson 1990; Okun 1984; Rawls 1971). The Center for the Study of Social Policy defines "equity" as "the effort to provide different levels of support based on an individual's or group's needs to achieve fairness in outcomes" (2019, 5).

Values can also be critically important to nonprofit performance, as the movement continues for nonprofits to function in a more "businesslike" manner (Cheverton 2007). Researchers have examined whether certain values can coexist (such as profit and social good). The rise of social entrepreneurship illustrates the realization that if businesses can articulate and commit to a larger purpose, a social purpose, they can make money while doing good. Social entrepreneurs have adapted the nonprofit values with a business for-profit purpose. While we could argue these two sets of values (public purpose and market orientation) may be at odds, there are for profit and nonprofit organizations combining these values (Toms Shoes n.d.). Ashoka is a 501(c)(3) nonprofit organization founded in 1981 to support social entrepreneurs around the world. Even though they are a traditional nonprofit in terms of tax status and public mission, they operate more like a for-profit company. They state their values on their website: belonging, optimism, inclusion, courage, and wisdom (Ashoka n.d.). While they do make all their financial information available on their website, there is no mention of their board of directors, the governing body of the nonprofit. Ashoka's founder, Bill Drayton, has been CEO of the organization since its inception 41 years ago. On the other hand, Toms Shoes is a for-profit company founded in 2006 by Blake Mycoskie, but creditors took over the company in 2019 from the founder. Toms's social-enterprise model meant they would donate a pair of shoes for each pair of shoes sold, a program that ended in 2019. The company moved to a more traditional grant model following criticism that the one-to-one model displaced local products and that the donated shoes were not high quality or appropriate for local environments (Ryan 2021). Social-enterprise businesses must produce profits, but nonprofits do not have the same bottom line. The measure of their success lies in their mission. "Nonprofits must create value within operational and environmental constraints that are at once more complex than those faced by corporations and more opaque than those confronted by government" (Frumkin and Andre-Clark 2000, 160).

Is it necessary to view nonprofits as a distinct form of organization, especially with the sectors blurring? Some research suggests that nonprofits are in fact distinct given their value of generating assistance at no cost, yet nonprofits must still adopt business and government practices to operate (Knusten 2012). Nonprofits are unique because of their engagement with volunteers and donors, where individuals give their resources freely without any expectation of something in return. Even paid staff often volunteer and donate because they are driven by a strong sense of mission and value alignment. In return, the organization serves the community, building up social capital. These unique abilities ensure self-sustainability (2012). The value produced by nonprofit organizations is the achievement of the mission through donations rather than (or in addition to) revenue from customers (Moore 2000).

Research suggests that tensions exist between certain values, especially between market or profit values and others. In a study of professional theatres, researchers found tensions between artistic-value dimensions and market-oriented values (Voss, Cable, and Voss 2000). If nonprofits are to compete against for-profits, which is common in the education and human-services subsectors, then they should capitalize on the values of the organization and the values of their donors, volunteers, and staff. By creating a distinctive set of values and demonstrating their performance, nonprofits can reconcile any tension and compete in the marketplace.

➤ case example #11

A relatively new organization wanted to undertake a strategic planning process for the first time. The staff and volunteers were particularly interested in getting some direction from the board after it asked them to offer new programs and expand their services. They felt they needed guidance because they seemed to be chasing opportunities in a variety of directions. In addition, a particular funding opportunity had appeared that could really take the organization to a new level. If successful, this funding would double their program revenue and provide opportunities for hundreds of people. Although not a permanent revenue source, it would be an infusion of needed cash and an opportunity to leverage other matching funds. The board was excited about the funding opportunity but cautious too, wondering if this was the right opportunity. During the strategic planning process, we spent time articulating, discussing, and reaching consensus on the organization's values. They were the foundation of the organization but had not been articulated before. In our discussions, we found there was strong agreement among the board and staff. Everyone was excited to have these guideposts based on values to rely on for decision-making. Clarifying the organization's values actually helped with the funding opportunity too. After this exercise, the board and staff understood that the funder did not align with their key values, and they decided not to pursue the opportunity. If they had and were successful, they could have faced some serious issues down the road.

⋀

Can values be used for organizational differentiation? We have seen the use of values in the competitive market of higher education.

The University of Phoenix used to be one of the largest for-profit colleges, but they quickly fell from grace. Their bottom-line for-profit status actually led to some of the highest student tuition costs, which led to staggering student-loan debt for their students. As a result, the University of Phoenix became the subject of a number of state and federal investigations for deceptive business practices, including false advertising and inappropriate financial-aid practices. The Federal Trade Commission (FTC) filed suit against the university, which resulted in a settlement of a $50 million payment to the FTC and cancellation of $141 million in student debt, monies owed to the school itself but not the money owed by students as part of federal loans (Federal Trade Commission 2019). While the demand for flexible and online education continued to grow, nonprofit colleges stepped in and reaped the benefits of the fall of Phoenix. Western Governors University and Southern New Hampshire University, both nonprofit colleges, sought to fill the void left by the University of Phoenix and used their nonprofit classification to distinguish themselves from other for-profit online colleges. In an article in *Inside Higher Education*, a higher education consulting firm confirmed that nonprofit status is identified with quality and trust, especially after the University of Phoenix failure (Kreighbaum 2018). This example illuminates how nonprofit organizations compete across all sectors (public, private, and nonprofit). Nonprofits are often trusted more, screened less, monitored less, granted more discretion, and awarded longer contracts with governments while at the same time achieving higher service quality, responsiveness to the government, and customer satisfaction compared to private businesses (Witesman and Fernandez 2013).

You might be wondering what the difference is between a code of ethics and a values statement. The National Council of Nonprofits noted that values are overarching, whereas a code of ethics shares only some of those values, particularly honesty, integrity, and transparency (n.d.). For advice or guidance on a code of ethics, a nonprofit can refer to its professional associations, such as the Association of Fundraising Professionals' Code of Ethical Standards (2014). The IRS encourages nonprofits to adopt a code of ethics to ensure they're acting in the best interest of the public. Specifically, a nonprofit is asked about their code of ethics on the IRS 990 form in Part VI: Governance, Management, and Disclosure Sections A and B. Section A contains a series of questions about the organization. Section B covers policies required by the Internal Revenue Code. Overall, these questions fall under the values of voluntary transparency and accountability. See the excerpt from the IRS 990 form below (fig. 20). In this way, nonprofits publicly disclose whether they're guided by a code of ethics, which is a sign of good governance to external stakeholders, including legislatures and the general public.

Related but distinct, organizational values are the foundation for nonprofits at all stages and all sizes. At the creation of a nonprofit, the founders may believe that the mission is the most important reason to create a new organization, but values are "the principles and philosophies that influence the way in which the mission is carried out" (Brothers and Sherman 2012, 16). As the organization grows, values can be used as guideposts to rely on to make decisions about further growth and new directions. Values need to be articulated first but then lived every day for them to truly serve as the organization's foundation.

To come up with its values, the organization can start with a long list and have each person individually circle the values they believe are most important to the organization. You can find several online sources for a list of values, such as Brené Brown's "Dare to Lead List of Values" (Brown 2020). Then the participants should prioritize the values they've circled. Next, each person can state their top three choices, while the facilitator writes them on a whiteboard or paper so everyone can see them. Once every person has participated, there will likely be four to six values that are mentioned most frequently. The group can then discuss the remaining values and try to come to a consensus.

Here are three examples of nonprofits' values expressed in different formats.

BoardSource's work is grounded in a fundamental belief that boards are critical to organizational success. Their members serve out of loyalty and responsibility to the organization's mission and

Section B. Policies *(This Section B requests information about policies not required by the Internal Revenue Code.)*

		Yes	No
10a	Did the organization have local chapters, branches, or affiliates?	10a	
b	If "Yes," did the organization have written policies and procedures governing the activities of such chapters, affiliates, and branches to ensure their operations are consistent with the organization's exempt purposes?	10b	
11a	Has the organization provided a complete copy of this Form 990 to all members of its governing body before filing the form?	11a	
b	Describe on Schedule O the process, if any, used by the organization to review this Form 990.		
12a	Did the organization have a written conflict of interest policy? *If "No," go to line 13*	12a	
b	Were officers, directors, or trustees, and key employees required to disclose annually interests that could give rise to conflicts?	12b	
c	Did the organization regularly and consistently monitor and enforce compliance with the policy? *If "Yes," describe on Schedule O how this was done*	12c	
13	Did the organization have a written whistleblower policy?	13	
14	Did the organization have a written document retention and destruction policy?	14	
15	Did the process for determining compensation of the following persons include a review and approval by independent persons, comparability data, and contemporaneous substantiation of the deliberation and decision?		
a	The organization's CEO, Executive Director, or top management official	15a	
b	Other officers or key employees of the organization	15b	
	If "Yes" to line 15a or 15b, describe the process on Schedule O. See instructions.		
16a	Did the organization invest in, contribute assets to, or participate in a joint venture or similar arrangement with a taxable entity during the year?	16a	
b	If "Yes," did the organization follow a written policy or procedure requiring the organization to evaluate its participation in joint venture arrangements under applicable federal tax law, and take steps to safeguard the organization's exempt status with respect to such arrangements?	16b	

FIGURE 20

Section of the IRS 990 Form

provide essential oversight and accountability to the organization's beneficiaries, donors, and the broader public. In carrying out our own mission, BoardSource embraces the following values: courage, collaboration, curiosity, and inclusiveness. (BoardSource n.d.)

- **Community**: We collaborate with our team and partners to exceptionally serve one another and our neighbors. We honor diversity and celebrate our unique gifts and perspectives.
- **Humility**: We are humble and self-aware. We know when to ask for and accept help.
- **Impact**: We create positive change by focusing on what's most important to our mission.
- **Empowerment**: We trust and support each other to get the job done and to do it well.
- **Accountability**: We take ownership for our performance and honor our commitments.
- **Transparency**: We share information, as appropriate, openly and honestly through candid conversation. (Northern Illinois Foodbank n.d.)
- **Excellence**: In all we do, we hold ourselves to the highest standards. We are committed to continuous learning and improvement.
- **Respect**: We recognize the dignity of all people. We offer others—and ourselves—patience, kindness, openness and forgiveness. We take responsibility for our actions.
- **Opportunity**: We support each other—our customers and their families, our colleagues, the community, the environment, and ourselves—in building a better life.
- **Justice**: We build and maintain equity through our work and our relationships with customers, employees, the environment, and the community. (The Lift Garage n.d.)

Vision

An organization's vision is a shared picture of where the organization is headed. Many nonprofits do not specifically express a vision, and it is not required when filing for nonprofit status. But it is perhaps even more important than the mission because it describes a future reality. The mission becomes the working definition of how to achieve that vision. Organizations are often confused about the two statements. As mentioned earlier, appreciative inquiry is a framework that can be used to create a shared vision focused on positive experiences (Barrett and Fry 2005). Here is an example to illustrate the difference between a vision and a mission.

> *Vision*: A world where people are valued for their unique gifts so they can achieve whatever they wish to the best of their abilities.
> *Mission*: To create opportunities and training for people with disabilities to pursue employment opportunities.

In this example, if the organization is focused on providing a service (training and opportunities) but cannot clearly articulate what its vision is (the expected long-term outcome), then they can provide their service, but the people they work with may never be employed. A vision relates to the organization's "why," as explained by Simon Sinek (2008; 2009) in his TED Talk and book.

Creating a vision statement is not only important to collectively think about the future, but it should inspire everyone in and outside the organization. It is the chance to dream big. A vision can be articulated as a series of statements, one concise statement, or a descriptive paragraph. Organizations are not bound by word count, only imagination. Here are some examples of possible formats.

> A world where everyone has a decent place to live. (Habitat for Humanity n.d.)

> For no one in Northern Illinois to be hungry. (Northern Illinois Food Bank n.d.)

- As a thriving not-for-profit business, The Lift Garage offers quality affordable auto repair for people who are on a path to a better future.
- Everyone connected with The Lift Garage is committed to respect one another, to quality in our work, and a living wage for our employees.

- Our friendly and hospitable staff offer people excellent customer service. We stand behind our repairs and the skills of our staff.
- Our well-kept garage and offices are furnished with the tools and equipment we need to do the job right.
- As a locally owned business, we work hard to be a good neighbor. When we make decisions, we ask: What is best for the people involved? What is best for our community? What is best for the health of the planet?
- We go the extra mile for customers. If a car repair is too big for us or a customer has another important need, we do our best to connect people with helpful resources in our community.
- Each day, the people of The Lift Garage feel thankful. We know that, together, we are repairing not just cars but lives: restoring hope and opportunity by helping people get to school and to jobs is an important step toward a more promising and secure future. (The Lift Garage n.d.)

DeKalb County History Center will explore the diverse stories that are part of our county's history; gather people together through exhibits, programs, and research; and inspire people to apply this knowledge to enlighten the decisions of tomorrow. DeKalb County History Center is also committed to building the capacity of local organizations by providing resources and opportunities for collaboration. (DeKalb County History Center n.d.)

➤ case example #12

A nonprofit organization has provided workforce training to people with disabilities in our community for several years. The mission of the organization was to offer programs and services to these individuals so they can work on job skills. The founders created the organization particularly for people who have aged out of the public-school system at 21 and are no longer actively involved in learning with their peers. This organization provides programs for them to create individual goals, whether that's related to finances or job tasks. Overall the program was doing well. There was positive feedback from participants and their families. Staff assessed positive development in participants' knowledge and skills. From a program perspective, the organization was meeting its mission. But they had not articulated a vision prior to a strategic planning process. What would the world look like if they achieved their mission? What difference did they want to make, and were they working toward that? Through several facilitated discussions with the staff and board, they reached the conclusion that despite having excellent outcomes for participants, their vision was actually about society recognizing every individual for their own unique abilities, especially in the workforce. Once that vision became apparent, they could more easily see that their mission should ultimately move toward the common vision. If they were going to reach that vision and start changing opinions in very real ways, they needed to think about different programs for potential employers.

Λ

To create your organization's vision, you could use the table below to get started.

How do nonprofits' visions differ from for-profit businesses' visions? Nonprofit organizations often have broad visions and missions. Some research suggests that visions look different in nonprofits

TABLE 6. VISION SKETCH

Area	Your organization today	Your vision: what your organization looks like 10 years from now
Programs, services		
Staff, volunteers		
Governance, board		
Finances		
Marketing, communications		
Physical assets, facilities, space		
Other		

compared to for-profit businesses, even if they're both engaged in entrepreneurial activities, such as social enterprises (Ruvio, Rosenblatt, and Hertz-Lazarowitz 2010). Social entrepreneurship can take place as for-profit activities in nonprofit organizations or as activities in for-profit companies that promote social causes. Researchers found that for-profit entrepreneurs are more conservative than nonprofit entrepreneurs, and entrepreneurial vision is more significant in nonprofit organizations than in businesses. Nonprofits communicate their vision more broadly to stakeholders than for-profit organizations, possibly because of the mutual dependence on their networks or emphasis on community rather than personal gain or profit motives (Thompson, Alvy, and Lees 2000).

Mission

When a nonprofit organization is formed and applies to incorporate and receive nonprofit charitable status, the key component of those applications is to provide the organization's mission statement (Internal Revenue Service n.d.). The mission expresses how the organization wants to reach their vision (Brothers and Sherman 2012). As discussed in chapter 1, establishing the purpose and mission of a nonprofit organization is the primary responsibility of the board (Ingram 2015). A nonprofit's mission can be used as a tool to manage and motivate employees as well. One study found that, in general, employees who believed in the organization's mission were more satisfied with their employment and were likely to stay at the organization (Brown and Yoshioka 2003). There is also research to suggest some linkages between mission statements and performance, especially measures of financial performance. The research seems to question the assumption that mission statements necessarily lead to better performance, even though there are some connections between mission statements with a focused geographic scope and administrative expenses, and those mission statements that focus on a particular client group may experience increases in contributions (Kirk and Nolan 2010).

Nonprofits compete in many areas, such as competing for staff recruitment and retention, competing with other nonprofits for contracts and grants, and competing with for-profit companies for fee-based revenue. A study of the American Red Cross found they faced competition from both businesses and nonprofits that provide similar services. "Differentiation that is good for margin is not likely to be consistent with mission, but within donative markets, this strategy may serve both margin and mission" (Chetkovich and Frumkin 2003). This study showed that competition is difficult to manage and can hurt a nonprofit's mission, especially for fee-based activities. Although there is pressure to compete for fee-based services, this could have negative consequences for the organization's mission. The same pressure is not there in competition among other nonprofit organizations (2003).

Missions also need to be managed. Even though missions are at the core of the work of nonprofits, sometimes organizations can be tempted to pursue activities outside their mission, which is referred to as "mission drift" (Jones 2007). As nonprofits bow to pressure to become more businesslike and continue to professionalize, they may be attracted to new funding revenue to bend their missions into new areas (Maier, Meyer, and Steinbereithner 2016). Mission drift can be caused by a variety of sources, such as unrelated business activities (Weisbrod 2004). Mission drift due to pursuing unrelated business income is not an unwarranted concern. Most earned-income strategies pursued by nonprofits do not actually add to the bottom line once expenses are subtracted (Foster and Bradach 2005). One way to combat mission drift due to pursuing social-enterprise opportunities is to make sure the organization is connecting with external stakeholders so the mission remains true to the core value of the organization (Ramus and Vaccaro 2017). Nonprofits also need to have internal processes in place to ensure staff can focus on organizational performance to avoid mission drift (Hersberger-Langloh, Stühlinger, and von Schnurbein 2020). In a study of nonprofit hospitals, a clear and motivating mission led to more innovation (McDonald 2007).

Another cause of mission drift is the possibility of funding from governments and foundations, and each group's own funding priorities and agendas. Both have vast financial resources to direct in any way they choose, and nonprofits must accept those priorities or raise revenue for their organizations in other ways (Jones 2007).

For new organizations, or those reviewing their mission statements, here is a series of questions to help guide the discussion.

- What is the result or change you want to impact?
- Is the mission written from the perspective of the organization (what we are going to do for you) or from the perspective of the individual or community you plan to serve? This matters, especially for performance measurement (see chapter 6). If organizations focus their mission from the perspective of those they serve, it may be more difficult to measure, but it focuses the organization on impact rather than the ability of the organization to deliver services.
- Who cares about the organization's mission? Who will benefit?
- Can you focus the mission statement in one simple sentence that anyone can understand?

You can test out several different versions of the mission statement and see how each resonates with the organization's stakeholders; but avoid the temptation to create one sentence "by committee." Try to avoid inserting words here and there to make one person happy. This kind of editing will likely result in a sentence that's too long and doesn't read well. As a final check, make sure the mission uses active and aspirational language. A mission statement is something that should be reviewed at least annually and should evolve over time.

Why Mission Statements Need to Evolve

Jane Addams opened Hull Settlement House in Chicago in 1889. Eventually about 35 other settlement houses provided necessary human services not offered by the government or other agencies, mainly to immigrant families. Over a century later, in 2012, Hull House closed its doors, and the 60,000 people it served annually had to go elsewhere. There are many reasons Hull House did not survive, but one critical piece is evident in the examination of its mission.

Jane Addams Hull House Association improves social conditions for underserved people and communities by providing creative, innovative programs and advocating for related public policy reforms. Jane Addams Hull House Association provides childcare, domestic violence counseling and prevention, economic development, family services, job training, literacy training, senior services, foster care, independent living, and housing assistance for 60,000 children, families and community members each year in communities in and around Chicago. Hull House also advocates for social and public policy reforms and initiatives that impact the lives of the men, women, and children in the communities we serve.

(Jane Addams Hull House Association 2008)

It had an expansive mission despite the proliferation of government and other nonprofit agencies with the same or similar missions and the creation of legislation at the federal, state, and local levels to assist those in need (Cohen 2012).

For comparison, here are some examples of good mission statements.

Together, we create life-changing wishes for children with critical illnesses. (Make-A-Wish n.d.)

Seeking to put God's love into action, Habitat for Humanity brings people together to build homes, communities, and hope. (Habitat for Humanity n.d.)

To improve children's lives by creating a community where play and learning connect. (Chicago Children's Museum n.d.)

It is possible for missions to become outdated when a founding board member or a long-serving administrator stymies innovation or change. If an organization's founder or a staff member remains involved in an organization over a long time, there is the potential for founder's syndrome in that their opinions and actions supersede others', which may not be in the best interest of the organization.

This chapter has shown the importance of values, vision, and mission to the overall sustainability of the organization—as well as their importance to innovation, employee satisfaction, and stakeholder trust. The board is the governing body of a nonprofit organization. The work on values, vision, and mission typically takes place in a retreat of the board or the strategic planning committee. If done in person, there are many activities that can help board members do a thorough review and reach consensus. Here are a couple of innovative products that may be useful for this work, especially if you decide to manage the strategic planning process without an outside facilitator.

- What's Worth Doing (Experience Institute n.d.) is a deck of cards created by the Experience Institute and their partners that helps individuals create a mind map based on three main questions: what challenges you want to address, what kind of people you enjoy working with, and what you like to make. The cards about challenges you want to address can be used as an individual or group exercise to visualize and think through the values, vision, and mission of an organization.
- Cards for Culture—Museum Edition (Cards for Culture n.d.) is a three-deck box of cards geared specifically to assist museums with strategy development. One deck of 64 cards contains strategy questions based on eight themes (story, leadership, audience, organization, community, society, space, and assets). Another deck of 16 cards examines external issues affecting museums. The final deck of 16 cards includes best practices from museums around the world. The cards work well with groups and, although made for museums, could be easily adapted for other arts-and-culture organizations.

DISCUSSION QUESTIONS

1. Why is an examination of an organization's values, vision, and mission an important component of a strategic planning process?
2. Why is it important for a nonprofit to have a values statement?
3. How do a vision and a mission differ from each other?

REFERENCES

Ashoka (n.d.). What Ashoka does. Accessed February 20, 2022. https://www.ashoka.org/en-us.

Association of Fundraising Professionals. (2014). Code of ethical standards. https://afpglobal.org/ethicsmain/code-ethical-standards.

Barrett, F., and Fry, R. (2005). *Appreciative Inquiry: A Positive Approach to Building Cooperative Capacity*. Chagrin Falls, OH: Taos Institute Publications.

BoardSource. (n.d.). Our vision, mission, and core values. Accessed February 20, 2022. https://boardsource.org/about-boardsource/vision-mission-core-values/.

Brothers, J., and Sherman, A. (2012). *Building Nonprofit Capacity: A Guide to Managing Change through Organizational Lifecycles*. Hoboken, NJ: John Wiley & Sons.

Brown, B. (2020). Dare to lead list of values. Accessed February 20, 2022. https://brenebrown.com/resources/dare-to-lead-list-of-values/.

Brown, W., and Yoshioka, C. (2003). Mission attachment and satisfaction as factors in employee retention. *Nonprofit Management and Leadership* 14(1): 5–18.

Cards for Culture. (n.d.). Playful strategy development for museums. Accessed February 20, 2022. https://www.kickstarter.com/projects/cardsforculture/cards-for-culture-playful-strategy-development-for.

Center for the Study of Social Policy. (2019). Key equity terms and concepts: A glossary for shared understanding. https://cssp.org/wp-content/uploads/2019/09/Key-Equity-Terms-and-Concepts-vol1.pdf.

Chen, K., Lune, H., and Quen, E. (2013). How values shape and are shaped by nonprofit and voluntary organizations: The current state of the field. *Nonprofit and Voluntary Sector Quarterly* 42(5): 856–885.

Chetkovich, C. and Frumkin, P. (2003). Balancing margin and mission: Nonprofit competition in charitable versus fee-based programs. *Administration and Society* 35(5): 564–596.

Cheverton, J. (2007). Holding our own: Value and performance in nonprofit organisations. *Australian Journal of Social Issues* 42(3): 427–436.

Chicago Children's Museum. (n.d.). About us. Accessed February 20, 2022. https://www.chicagochildrensmuseum.org/about-us.

Cohen, R. (2012). Death of the Hull House: A nonprofit coroner's inquest. *Nonprofit Quarterly*. https://nonprofitquarterly.org/hull-house-death-nonprofit-coroners-inquest/.

DeKalb County History Center. (n.d.). About us. Accessed February 20, 2022. https://www.dekalbcountyhistory.org/about-us/.

Drucker, P. (1990). *Managing the Nonprofit Organization*. New York: Harper-Collins.

Experience Institute. (n.d.). What's Worth Doing? Accessed February 20, 2022. https://store.expinstitute.com/products/whats-worth-doing-pre-sale.

Federal Trade Commission. (2019). FTC obtains record $191 million settlement from University of Phoenix to resolve FTC charges it used deceptive advertising to attract prospective students. https://www.ftc.gov/news-events/press-releases/2019/12/ftc-obtains-record-191-million-settlement-university-phoenix.

Foster, W., and Bradach, J. (2005). Should nonprofits seek profits? *Harvard Business Review* 83(2): 92–100.

Frederickson, H. (1990). Public administration and social equity. *Public Administration Review* 50: 228–237.

Frumkin, P., and Andre-Clark, A. (2000). When missions, markets, and politics collide: Values and strategy in the nonprofit human services. *Nonprofit and Voluntary Sector Quarterly* 29(1): 141–163.

Habitat for Humanity. (n.d.). Our mission, vision and principles. Accessed February 20, 2022. https://www.habitat.org/about/mission-and-vision.

Hersberger-Langloh, S., Stühlinger, S., and von Schnurbein, G. (2020). Institutional isomorphism and nonprofit managerialism: For better or worse? *Nonprofit Management and Leadership* 31(3): 1–20.

Ingram, R. (2015). Ten basic responsibilities of nonprofit boards. BoardSource. https://boardsource.org/product/ten-basic-responsibilities-nonprofit-boards/.

Internal Revenue Service. (n.d.). Applying for tax exempt status. Accessed February 20, 2022. https://www.irs.gov/charities-non-profits/applying-for-tax-exempt-status.

Jane Addams Hull House Association. (2008). IRS Form 990.

Jeavons, T. (1992). When the management is the message: Relating values to management practice in nonprofit organizations. *Nonprofit Management and Leadership* 2(4): 403–417.

Jones, M. (2007). The multiple sources of mission drift. *Nonprofit and Voluntary Sector Quarterly* 36(2): 299–307.

Joyaux, S. (2015). Values in your organization and what they have to do with making money: Part 2. *Nonprofit Quarterly*. September 11, 2015. https://nonprofitquarterly.org/values-in-your-organization-and-what-they-have-to-do-with-making-money-part-2/.

Kirk, G., and Nolan, S. (2010). Nonprofit mission statement focus and financial performance. *Nonprofit Management and Leadership* 20(4): 473–490.

Knutsen, W. (2012). Value as a self-sustaining mechanism: Why some organizations are different from and similar to private and public organizations. *Nonprofit and Voluntary Sector Quarterly* 42(5): 985–1005.

Kreighbaum, A. (2018). More pressure on accreditors in changing higher ed landscape. *Inside Higher Education*. August 14, 2018. https://www .insidehighered.com/news/2018/08/15/accreditors-pressured-apply -more-scrutiny-profits-look-change-tax-status.

Maier, F., Meyer, M., and Steinbereithner, M. (2016). Nonprofit organizations becoming business-like: A systematic review. *Nonprofit and Voluntary Sector Quarterly* 45(1): 64–86.

Make-A-Wish. (n.d.). Our mission. Accessed February 20, 2022. https:// wish.org/mission.

McDonald, R. (2007). An investigation of innovation in nonprofit organizations: The role of organizational mission. *Nonprofit and Voluntary Sector Quarterly* 36(2): 256–281.

Moore, M. (2000). Managing for value: Organizational strategy in for-profit, nonprofit, and governmental organizations. *Nonprofit and Voluntary Sector Quarterly* 29(1): 183–204.

National Council of Nonprofits. (n.d.). Code of ethics for nonprofits— Why your nonprofit may want to adopt a statement of values. Accessed February 20, 2022. https://www.councilofnonprofits.org/tools-resources /code-of-ethics-nonprofits-why-your-nonprofit-may-want-adopt -statement-of-values.

Northern Illinois Food Bank. (n.d.). Our mission. Accessed February 20, 2022. https://solvehungertoday.org/about-us/our-mission/.

Okun, A. (1984). *The Big Tradeoff*. Washington, DC: Brookings Institution.

Ramus, R., and Vaccaro, A. (2017). Stakeholders matter: How social enterprises address mission drift. *Journal of Business Ethics* 143: 307–322.

Rawls, J. (1971). *A Theory of Justice*. Cambridge, MA: Harvard University Press.

Rothschild, J., and Milofksy, C. (2006). The centrality of values, passions, and ethics in the nonprofit sector. *Nonprofit Management and Leadership* 17(2): 137–143.

Ruvio, A., Rosenblatt, Z., and Hertz-Lazarowitz, R. (2010). Entrepreneur-ial leadership vision in nonprofit vs. for-profit organizations. *The Leadership Quarterly* 21(1): 144–158.

Ryan, T. (2021). Toms finds one-for-one charitable model doesn't add up for its business. Retail Wire. April 13, 2021. https://retailwire.com /discussion/toms-finds-one-for-one-charitable-model-doesnt-add-up -for-its-business/.

Sinek, S. (2008). How great leaders inspire action. TEDxPuget Sound. September 29, 2008. https://www.ted.com/talks/simon_sinek_how _great_leaders_inspire_action?language=en.

Sinek, S. (2009). *Start with Why: How Great Leaders Inspire Everyone to Take Action*. New York: Portfolio.

Stackhouse, M. L. (1990). Religion and the social space for voluntary institutions. In *Faith and Philanthropy in America: Exploring the Role of Religion in America's Voluntary Sector*, edited by R. Wuthnow and V. Hodgkinson, 22–37. Hoboken, NJ: Jossey-Bass.

Svara, J., and Brunet, J. (2005). Social equity is a pillar of public administration. *Journal of Public Affairs Education* 11(3): 253–258.

Svara, J., and Brunet, J. (2020). The importance of social equity to prevent a hollow public administration. *American Review of Public Administration* 59(4–5): 352–357.

The Lift Garage. (n.d.). Mission, vision, and values. Accessed February 20, 2022. https://www.theliftgarage.org/about/.

Thomspon, J., Alvy, G., and Lees, A. (2000). Social entrepreneurship—A new look at the people and potential. *Management Decision* 38: 343–377.

Toms Shoes. (n.d.). (Website). Accessed February 20, 2022. https://www .toms.com/.

Voss, G., Cable, D., and Voss, Z. (2000). Linking organizational values to relationships with external constituents: A study of nonprofit theatres. *Organizational Science* 11(3): 330–347.

Weisbrod, B. (2004). The pitfalls of profits. *Stanford Social Innovation Review* 2(3): 40–47.

Witesman, E. and Fernandez, S. (2013). Government contracts with private organizations: Are there differences between nonprofits and for-profits? *Nonprofit and Voluntary Sector Quarterly* 42(4): 689–715.

Wooldridge, B. (1998). Protecting equity while reinventing government: Strategies for achieving a "fair" distribution of the costs and benefits of the public sector. *Journal of Public Management and Social Policy* 4(1): 67–80.

CHAPTER 6

Performance Measurement

KEY CONCEPTS
- Outputs versus outcomes
- Factors affecting adoption of performance measurement
- Performance measurement versus performance management
- Challenges in measuring nonprofit performance
- Efficiency versus effectiveness (double bottom line)
- Social, environmental, and financial performance (triple bottom line)
- Logic models or theories of change

"Performance measurement" and "performance management" are not new terms, but they continue to evolve in their application to the nonprofit sector and vary a great deal across different types of nonprofits. Although some have called for nonprofits to be more businesslike, it's still unclear how accountability for performance can be accomplished (e.g., Dart 2004). Accountability for government has been defined by a few scholars. Metzenbaum (2005) identified four categories of accountability expectations: fiscal, ethical, democratic, and performance. Behn (2000) focused on three areas: finances, fairness, and performance. He argued that traditional public adminis-

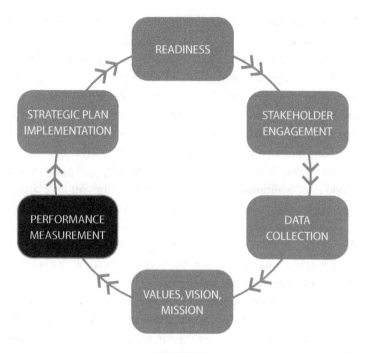

FIGURE 21
Cycle of Strategic Planning

tration focuses on finances (equity) and fairness (equality) but less so on performance. Finances and fairness are process and results oriented and are easier to measure than performance. Finances and fairness can also be at odds with performance; therefore, it's difficult to articulate and agree on the elements of quality performance in the public sector (2000). For nonprofits, we could argue there is still an expectation for fiscal, ethical, and performance accountability. To monitor nonprofits' accountability, we have procedural, legal, and regulatory mechanisms. Government requires that only nonprofit organizations (with some exceptions) of a certain size disclose certain information in audited financial statements and the IRS 990 form, the primary disclosure document for nonprofits. If we examine audited financial statements (which not all nonprofits are required to have), we see the line items don't contain any information about program effectiveness; so we still need more information. Charity watchdogs like

Charity Navigator and Better Business Bureau can only rate a fraction of the nonprofits that exist in the US. Besides mandatory financial statements, IRS 990 forms, and information provided by third-party watchdog groups identified above, we are left with voluntary performance reporting by nonprofit organizations. While the private sector can look to their profits and growth as a measure of performance, the nonprofit-sector measures are not easily captured.

Since the late 1960s, public services are more likely to be provided via contracts with nonprofit organizations than by public employees; in addition, traditional government grants to nonprofits have largely been replaced with performance contracts (Boris et al. 2010; Smith 2010; Martin 2002; Salamon 2002; Gordon 2001; Marin 2001). Because government contracts are an important source of revenue for nonprofit organizations, those that have contracted with a government have increased the requirements for performance data to maintain the performance contracts (Gazley 2008). In addition to the government, other funders like the United Way have encouraged performance measurement in their funded agencies since the late 1990s. Around this time, nonprofit organizations were adopting the balanced-scorecard system, a model of performance measurement used in the private and public sectors (Kaplan 2001).

Adoption of Performance Measurement

Funding, including opportunities found in federated funds, foundations, or government grants, is often the impetus for a nonprofit organization to adopt a performance-measurement system. Over 15 years ago, United Way issued its first guide for outcome measurement. Researchers have found that larger nonprofits, those in certain subsectors, and those that receive federal funding or funding from the United Way are more likely to implement performance measurement (Salamon 2012; Carman 2009; Gronbjerg 1993). Organizations that are part of a national alliance, coalition, or network are likely familiar with such a program, one in which periodic assessment is required to remain affiliated with the national association or federation. Small-town hospitals, substance-abuse clinics, soup kitchens, and hospice organizations, however, are also experiencing pressure to engage in ongoing evaluation and outcomes measurement to demonstrate their quality of service to clients (Slatten, Guidry, and Austin 2011).

Although funders' outcome-measurement requirements affect the use of outcome measurement by nonprofit organizations, we don't fully understand the context in which the adoption of these practices occurs (Thomson 2010). Age of the organization has a positive relationship with the use of performance information. Older nonprofits have likely learned how to best use their resources, have achieved a certain level of stability in funding, and have leadership focused on long-term objectives. The age of an organization is also indicative of a strong governance structure and solid management practices that are likely to lead to higher levels of performance-measurement adoption. Specifically, the age of organizations has a positive association with the extent to which organizations use benchmarks for measuring program outcomes or results and the extent to which organizations integrate performance information into their budget-preparation process (Carman and Fredericks 2010; Light 2004; Connelly and York 2003; Simon 2001). Other factors contributing to performance-information use were found in an analysis of 25 recently published studies of performance measurement: measurement-system maturity, stakeholder involvement, leadership support, support capacity, innovative culture (see chapter 2), and goal clarity (Kroll 2015).

Double Bottom Line

Researchers break down the term "performance accountability" into two dimensions: efficiency (of resources expended to produce the desired impact) and effectiveness (achieving the intended results). This dual concept is sometimes referred to as the "double bottom line" (Kushner and Pool 1996; Martin and Kettner 1996). Because nonprofits have an obligation to disclose both financial information

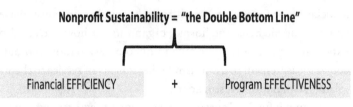

Nonprofit Sustainability = "the Double Bottom Line"

Financial EFFICIENCY	+	Program EFFECTIVENESS

Money:
- Are we managing our resources for maximum efficiency?
- Are we getting enough financial return/profitability to continue?
- How do we measure this?

Mission:
- Are we meeting our program goals and objectives (inputs, outputs, outcomes)?
- Are we having an impact on our mission?
- How do we measure this?

FIGURE 22
Efficiency vs. Effectiveness

that focuses on efficiency and program information that focuses on effectiveness, they're clearly subject to this double bottom line (Rosenzweig 2004; Illinois Facilities Fund and Donors Forum of Chicago 1998; Weisbrod 1998). Financial disclosure could include the IRS 990 form, financial statements on the organization's website, and the release of more relevant information to stakeholders, including program outcomes (Keating and Frumkin 2003). Researchers have concluded, however, that we "should move away from concepts and measures of efficiency based on financial ratios, and toward ones that embrace maximizing what nonprofits are able to make and do" (Coupet and Berrett 2019, 299). Balancing the two dimensions of the double bottom line is not easy though. See the figure above for questions to consider.

Triple Bottom Line

The notion of a triple bottom line comes from the business literature, and it divides performance along three dimensions: economic (financial), social (mission), and environmental. There are no universal definitions, however. Most researchers include the third aspect, environmental, as the third dimension of performance (Dart and

Hill 2010). Researchers have examined these three dimensions in studies of nonprofit community gardens (Stephenson, Brock, and Loughead 2008) and nonprofit arts organizations (Schiffer 2021). But Wyszomirski (2013) defines the triple bottom line of nonprofit arts organizations as financial, public value (mission), and "artistic vitality." Bratt (2012), on the other hand, extends the triple bottom line to the quadruple bottom line for nonprofit affordable-housing organizations (including financial, social, and environmental dimensions, as well as how the housing contributes to neighborhood viability). Some researchers suggest the triple bottom line can be misleading and can in fact be a "smokescreen," meaning organizations may use this language for marketing purposes without tying it to actual practices (Norman and MacDonald 2004). Other researchers suggest that organizational performance goes beyond financial and program measures to include the internal operation perspective and the innovative and learning perspective, suggesting a balanced scorecard with four quadrants instead of just two (Kaplan 2001; Kaplan and Norton 1992). A slight variation to the balanced-scorecard approach is called the "public value scorecard" (Moore 2003).

Another question researchers have tried to answer is whether donors even care about efficiency and effectiveness measures. Analyzing data from arts and culture nonprofit organizations, researchers found no evidence that performance affects an organization's ability to attract donations (Charles and Kim 2016). There is a relationship between capacity, revenue sources, operational activities, and measuring organizational effectiveness. In this model, organizational capacity refers to the financial and non-financial resources an organization has and the ways the organization tries to achieve its mission (Bryan 2019).

Scholars differentiate between the adoption of performance-measurement systems and their use in decision-making (implementation). Implementation is influenced by political and cultural factors (De Lancer Julnes and Holzer 2001). Further, the lack of investment in technology hinders the development and use of performance-measurement systems (Carman and Fredericks 2010; Connelly and York 2003). Researchers also found that organizations that support employee learning and development activities are more likely to collect performance data (Umar and Hassan 2019). The relationship depends, however, on the nonprofit's capacity to conduct performance assessment and the clarity of the organization's goals (2019).

Challenges

Some researchers suggest the problem is that nonprofits cannot implement and maintain performance-measurement systems. Nonprofits ignore capacity building, such as adding data-analysis responsibilities, because they deliberately invest in program delivery rather than organizational capacity; or, even if they want to tackle capacity building, they lack the knowledge to do so (Morino and Jonas 2001). Organizations receive signals from the public and funders to direct their dollars toward program and service delivery instead of systems and processes like data and technology that could ultimately improve efficiency and effectiveness.

Despite the use of performance measurement in many nonprofit organizations, significant challenges remain. Researchers have identified several contextual and process barriers to measuring the efficiency and effectiveness of nonprofits (Moxham and Boaden 2007). First, because funding is short term (one year or less), nonprofit organizations tend to be focused on short-term goals rather than long-term goals, which is an obstacle to long-term performance measurement (Morino and Jonas 2001). Second, measuring impact over time requires keeping in touch with stakeholders, which may not be possible because the services offered are confidential. A third barrier is the lack of common understanding and definitions of performance-measurement terms, such as "output" or "outcome," both within the organization and among external funders. Even among nonprofits, there is a lack of clarity in the terminology used by these organizations (Moxham 2010).

There are many reasons why measuring performance in nonprofits is challenging. Nonprofits measure their performance in terms of outputs only, as demanded by their funders. Measures can be unclear, and it can be difficult to connect the mission of the organization to its activities. Overall, feedback is not built into the system, and the measures being reported back to funders may not even be valid (Moxham and Boaden 2007). Few data about the impact of performance-measurement systems are available in the nonprofit sector (2007). Often nonprofits report their impact as dollars spent or services provided rather than the reach of their programs (Keating and Frumkin 2003).

Is there an alternative explanation, other than problems with nonprofit organizational capacity, for why performance accountability is not widely adopted by nonprofits? Perhaps it's that "nonprofits also must respond to the competing informational demands from multiple stakeholders, which limits the amount of resources nonprofits are willing to invest in one area of accountability" (Rivenbark and Menter 2006, 259). This sets up a classic principal-agent problem in which a principal hires an agent with the necessary skills to carry out a function that may be too costly or complex for the principal to handle alone. In this case, local government is the principal, and nonprofit organizations are the agents. Actions based on the principal-agent theory, however, complicate accountability for public funds. Nonprofits respond to the demands of the funder or, put another way, are at the mercy of funder accountability requirements to maintain funding (Moore 2003). The struggle for nonprofits then is managing different accountability requirements for different funders, including governments (Gazley 2010). The goal is for nonprofits to create outcome measurements that meet the internal needs of staff and information needs of external stakeholders (Rivenbark and Menter 2006).

Regardless of the type of performance-measurement system, larger questions remain, such as how performance measurement in the nonprofit sector contributes to or supports nonprofit accountability to their various stakeholders. Moxham and Boaden (2007), in their empirical case study, identified several contextual and processual barriers to measuring the efficiency and effectiveness of nonprofit organizations. They found that all four organizations they looked at were measuring performance in terms of outputs, which were demanded by their funders. Some nonprofits did measure inputs such as the number of paid staff and other resources. There were no common definitions of performance-measurement terms like "outputs," "outcomes," and "impact." None of the four organizations had clear performance objectives or goals, even though they all had defined quantitative measures (2007). "Financial measures may effectively capture the key risk and return measures of for-profit organizations. However, the contribution of nonprofits is not measured by the dollars spent on program services, but the reach of its programs" (Keating and Frumkin 2003). Performance inputs and outputs are useful to track, but reporting outcome measures is considerably more telling.

Performance reporting is further complicated by the fact that some nonprofits fund other nonprofits, such as community foundations. In effect, they act as funding intermediaries, defined as organizations that "gather funds from a range of public and private donors and re-grant these monies to a defined set of local nonprofits" (Benjamin 2010). Measuring performance of foundations is difficult given that "foundations work at the edges of large-scale social change rather than cause those changes in the first place" (Prewitt 2006). In another study, a public foundation developed a performance framework for its grantees to use but not for itself to base funding decisions upon (Benjamin 2010). The foundation used performance measurement and evaluation not to demonstrate the effectiveness of the foundation but rather to demonstrate the work of their grantees. Foundations are not honestly evaluating their contributions to broad social issues such as poverty eradication, disease elimination, and general quality of life. They support the organizations that go out there and do the work, but do not actually do the work themselves, which makes accounting for their performance more difficult.

Other types of nonprofits face similar challenges in using performance data. In a study of human-service organizations, researchers found these organizations collect data because they are needed by funders such as government agencies, but the data are not used to inform decision-making or improve performance (Kim, Charles, and Pettijohn 2019). To rectify this, the researchers argue that funders and nonprofits should work together to create meaningful performance measures so they can "meet both accountability and performance improvement aims" (2019).

⋗ case example #13

Funding organizations face challenges when reporting their own outcomes because these are dependent on the work of others. Second, their funding may only partially fund a particular program; as a result, their dollars aren't contributing in a major way to the organization's results overall. In one such case, a funder heard feedback from their funded agencies when they moved to outcome requirements for grants. Through a strategic planning process for the funder, the consultant met one-on-one with funded agencies to get their input. The agencies wouldn't likely share their challenges directly with the funder for fear that would be perceived as a negative signal, which would therefore reduce their funding. So the consultant's conversations were kept confidential to encourage the funded agencies to be honest and open. Based on these interviews, the funding organization decided to step back from strategic planning for a few months and instead focus on revising their grant-reporting requirements. Not only did the funder better understand their requirements from the agency perspective, but the organizations felt heard and were more likely to engage in the future.

⋏

As discussed earlier, even though performance measurement is encouraged in nonprofit organizations, several factors affect their adoption and use of performance measurement (Moxham and Boaden 2007; De Lancer Julnes and Holzer 2001). While boards and staff may not understand how to begin measuring their work, as Gazley and Kissman (2015, 5) point out, "Governance leaders can benefit from understanding theories of change generally."

Strategic planning and the process of data collection and goal setting require nonprofits to understand where they are and where they want to be. To accomplish that, an organization must have a strong performance culture that not only adopts performance measurement but, more importantly, adopts a performance-management philosophy and culture. What's the difference? Measurement is just measuring. But management means using the data to inform decision-making. You can't do performance management without the data, but data alone isn't enough. Many guides out there can help, but one of the better ones on performance measurement and management was produced by the US Department of Health and Human Services (2011). As you consider these concerns, keep this observation in mind: "What distinguishes the context for management in a values-expressive organization is that how the organization goes about setting and attaining specific goals becomes as important as the goals themselves" (Jeavons 1992, 409).

In Practice

The most challenging aspect of creating strategic goals for an organization is truly understanding how your organization is carrying out its mission and then working toward a shared vision. In this book, I've outlined the research and practice of engaging with stakeholders; the collection of data to determine the organization's strengths, weaknesses, opportunities, and threats; the evaluation of values, vision, and mission; and now performance measurement—all of which should lead to a better strategic plan. But to get across the finish line, several steps still lie ahead.

The second challenge when setting strategic goals is determining which issues are strategic and which are operational. Strategic goals cover the issues that are complex, longer-term (over 12 months to achieve), beyond the day-to-day operation of the organization, and require additional or re-reallocation of resources. Strategic goals are also not the status quo. If you just want to continue what you're doing and how you're doing it, you don't need a strategic plan. Just carry on. But if the organization wants to achieve more and to direct time and energy toward a specific destination in the future, then it will need to create bold and clear strategic goals to get there.

$\succ$ case example #14

An organization had gone through strategic planning in the past, several times in fact. The board was confident in their process and expected a similar experience. While this situation was encouraging, a review of previous plans revealed they were not strategic but rather contained vague goals covering all the programs offered without any timeline. In essence, the organization had been committing to doing the exact same thing they'd done for the past ten years without examining changes in context, resources, or demand for those services. During the strategic planning process, the board came to realize how much effort it took to truly examine why you do what you do, how you know you're doing it well, and what you're doing to reach your desired vision. While the overall positivity may have decreased in the short term, the organization ended up with a plan and goals that were clear, articulate, measurable, and aspirational. The staff were reenergized and the board more invested in the organization.

$\bigwedge$

To move toward the actual creation of a strategic plan, there are several steps at this stage of the process. Organizations can start by using a logic-model approach. Later in the chapter, I've included a worksheet based on this approach (figure 23). The Bridgespan Group also provides several helpful resources (Waldron et al. 2020). But let's break down the remaining steps here.

1. **Issue statement:** To clearly articulate the problem your work is trying to solve—that is, to frame a particular challenge for the population you serve—create an issue statement. This statement should briefly explain what needs to change: why is there a need for an intervention? Include "who, what, why, where, when," and "how" in your statement. Issue statements should address a particular weakness or opportunity identified in your data-collection stage (see chapter 4) that clearly aligns with

your organization's values, vision, and mission. For the purposes of strategic planning, after consulting with dozens of nonprofit organizations, I've concluded that strategic issues fall into six broad categories.

- **Financial**: Fund balances, debt, operating deficits, and fundraising
- **Governance**: Board, legal, and staff relations
- **Physical assets**: Facilities and capital improvements
- **Human resources**: Volunteers and staff, and succession
- **Programs and services**: Hours, locations, and partnerships
- **Marketing and communications**: Social media, print campaigns, and advocacy

2. **Goal**: Next, think about your overall purpose. What are you trying to accomplish? The answer to this question is the solution to your issue statement and will serve as your goal. There are whole books dedicated to performance measurement in nonprofit organizations, such as *The Nonprofit Outcomes Toolbox* (Penna 2011), *Impact and Excellence* (Chaney Jones 2014) and *The Goldilocks Challenge* (Gugerty and Karlan 2018). These as well as other resources are all very useful, especially when you start defining the issues the organization wants to address in its strategic plan. The data collection you did (see chapter 5) helps the organization define where it currently is so you can create measurable goals for the future. We often hear the term "SMART goals," which stands for specific, measurable, achievable, realistic, and timely. These terms are useful when crafting any strategic goals because they focus the organization. You can have one or more goals under each of these issues, depending generally on the size of the organization both in budget and staff. The larger and more complex the organization, the more strategic goals it might have.

The challenge is to create a strategic plan that is realistic but also inspiring.

- **Financial**: Financial goals are often easy to create because you have clear financial information, such as a budget or financial statements. An example of a goal in the financial category might be "to increase the percentage of operating revenue from grants from 5% to 10% by 2025." This is clear and measurable because you know exactly where the organization is starting from (5% of total revenue is currently coming from grants), and you know where you want to go. What is not useful is creating goals not based on the current situation or based on an undefined future condition—for example, "continue to improve fundraising efforts." Someone reading that goal has no idea where the organization currently is nor what it needs to do to achieve that goal going forward.

- **Governance**: This issue refers to anything to do with board oversight, legal authority, or board and staff relations. For example, a goal in this category could be "to evaluate the board nomination process so we can create a diverse board-member recruitment strategy by December 2022." This goal is part process (evaluation), but it also incorporates a specific product (recruitment strategy) and has a specific timeline.

- **Physical assets**: The organization may or may not own buildings or property, but all organizations own records and equipment and maybe have inventory or other assets they are responsible for. Goals in this category may include goals about managing those assets, changing those assets, or even selling those assets. For example, a goal could be "to research and secure a new office location closer to downtown at a lower annual occupancy cost than the current building by May 2024."

- **Human resources**: Since nonprofit organizations provide services, their single greatest asset is the people who deliver those services. These can be paid employees or volunteers. Several possible goals fall into this issue, ranging from staff succession plans to employee professional development, employee health care, volunteer recruitment and recognition, and so on. An example of a goal could be "to add two staff members in the development department to support the launch of a capital campaign by July 2023."

- **Programs and services**: Since this is the main source of mission attainment, the issue of programs and services is of critical importance in any nonprofit strategic plan. Goals in this category could relate to the program participants, location of programs, collaborative agreements with other agencies to deliver services, or a number of other issues. It is most important that data drive the decision-making here since this work is directly related to mission. It is easy to write goals such as "continue to provide high-quality service," but that goal is not SMART or even strategic—it begs the question, when would you stop providing high-quality service? To avoid this kind of vagueness, use the information you gathered (see chapter 4) to craft goals that will address any gaps in service, a desire to expand or increase services, a focus on a new service population, or a desire to grow into a new physical territory or location. There is pressure from donors, funders, and the general public for nonprofits to clearly articulate the impact they are having with the people they serve and the broader community. Program outcomes are much harder to measure, although it can be done. It does take dedication to gather data not just for data's sake, but rather to be truly responsive to the people you serve and to measure the outcomes not only in the short term but in the long term as well. Outcomes should be measured at the smallest unit (the individual level) because then those results can be aggregated to the program or organizational level as needed.

- **Marketing and communications:** Items in this area generally consist of internal and external communications such as social media, print campaigns, advocacy, a website, print and digital materials, and branding. Sometimes these responsibilities are part of staff roles; other times, in smaller organizations, they are contracted out to a private company, or volunteers and interns are used. In any case, clear goals for marketing and communications are important. Marketing and communications support revenue (such as fundraising campaigns), participant recruitment, and staff retention, among many other issues. In general, nonprofits underinvest in marketing and communications efforts, which negatively affects the organization. An example of a goal in this category that's not strategic is "grow our online presence." An example of a SMART goal would be "measure and capture data of all 2,500 program participants from 2012 to 2020 in our fundraising database by July 2022." There are many measurable and specific goals for marketing and communications, from simply looking at the metrics of followers or likes to more complex analyses of the depth of online engagement.

3. **Inputs:** Identify the available resources for your program. This helps you determine the extent to which you'll be able to implement the program and achieve your goals and outcomes. List the resources you **currently have** to support your program. (If you intend to raise additional resources during this program time frame, account for

them under "Activities.") Types of resources include the following.

- **Human resources**: Full- and part-time staff, consultants (e.g., in fundraising, technical support, strategic planning, communications), pro bono staff services, and volunteers
- **Financial resources**: Restricted grants, operating budget, and other monetary resources
- **Space**: Office and other facilities
- **Technology**: Computer hardware and software, and communication infrastructure (email, website)
- **Other equipment**: Office machinery (printers, copiers) and equipment specific to the program
- **Materials and other**: Office supplies, program materials (training materials), insurance, and so on.

4. **Outputs**: Outputs are the measurable, tangible, and direct products or results of program activities. They lead to desired outcomes—benefits for participants, families, communities, or organizations—but are not themselves the changes you expect the program will produce. An output statement does not reveal anything about **quality**. You will assess the quality of your outputs in your evaluation. Outputs frequently include **quantities** or reflect the existence of something new. Examples of program outputs include the **number and descriptions** of the number of home-buying workshops attended, the number of neighborhoods researched, the number of program participants served, or the hours of service provided. Make sure the outputs have activities and resources associated with them. This is one way a logic model is useful—to check whether a program has planned how it will create a product or deliver a service.

5. **Outcomes**: Outcomes express the results that the program intends to achieve if implemented as planned. Outcomes are the **changes that occur** or the **difference that is made** for individuals, groups, families, organizations,

systems, or communities during or after the program. Outcomes answer the questions, "What difference does the program make? What does success look like?" They reflect the core achievements you hope for with the program. Outcomes begin with the alignment of the organization's values, vision, and mission (see chapter 5) and then require determining a theory of change or logic model that visually demonstrates the impact the organization wants to have (Knowlton and Phillips 2009). You can begin by taking each program the organization provides and determining the short-term output goal and the long-term outcome goal.

6. **Logic model**: Finally, assemble all the pieces into a logic model. Below is a template you can use to visually depict what you want to achieve in one program. You can also use the template for the organization as a whole.

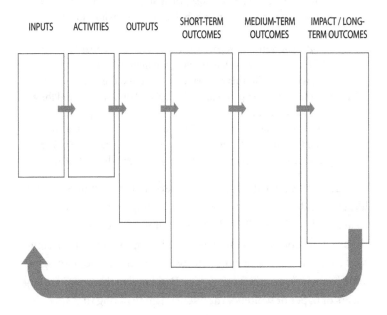

FIGURE 23
Logic Model Worksheet

By this point, you should have a clear set of issues with one or more strategic goals under each that address that issue. Those goals should be transferred into a logic model. Keep in mind, not every goal must have measurable outcomes. These worksheets then become your list of possible goals, but the work isn't over yet. Next comes prioritizing the goals to select the final goals for the current strategic plan. This is the challenging part of the process, especially if the organization is trying to do this without external support or a facilitator. If the staff have been leading the process, then the board will naturally want to take on as many strategic goals as possible since they envision the staff being the ones to implement the plan. It's human nature to be overly optimistic about what can be accomplished in a reasonable time frame. Here are some suggestions to deal with this scenario.

- When the goals have all been created and a rough timeline developed for each one, start a fresh timeline on paper or online that begins with the end in mind. Ask yourself, "To accomplish each goal by the date we chose, what steps do we need to take between now and then to reach that goal, and who will do that work?"
- Another option is to separate each goal and, in a board retreat or follow-up meeting, have each board member select one goal they will lead. Do this anonymously first and then have everyone physically go up to that goal, displayed on a whiteboard for instance, and put their name next to it. If everyone's names are crowded beside three out of seven goals, for example, this should prompt a discussion about how important the other goals are when no board member wants to lead those efforts.

Generally, retreats work best in person, but with interruptions like the pandemic and travel sometimes being a problem, online retreats can be effective. The challenge online is that the tools need to change. One option is to use an online platform specifically designed for collaboration such as Mural (https://www.mural.co/). Imagine a large room where a group can gather. Displayed in that room are large sheets of paper or whiteboards. Now imagine taking that space into a digital format. That is Mural. It can be used for highly engaging icebreakers and offers a number of templates to engage a group online in real time using digital sticky notes and other tools. The cost is calculated on a sliding scale based on the number of users.

The overall purpose of these exercises is to create clear strategic goals and to "right-size" the strategic plan. Regardless of how many goals the group has come up with, each one will need to be managed—and it's important that the plan isn't overly ambitious. No one wants to report on goals that haven't started to be addressed or spend too much time monitoring goals that haven't been given enough time and resources to be accomplished. Right-sizing the plan is important as the organization moves on to the next stage, which is implementation.

DISCUSSION QUESTIONS

1. What is the difference between an output and an outcome?
2. Why is it important for a board to understand a program's theory of change or logic model?
3. What factors drive adoption of performance measurement in nonprofit organizations?
4. What is the tension between financial efficiency and program effectiveness?
5. Is the triple bottom line a concept your organization should consider?
6. Why do strategic goals need to be SMART?

REFERENCES

Behn, R. (2000). *Rethinking Democratic Accountability*. Washington, DC: Brookings Institution.

Benjamin, L. (2010). Mediating accountability: How nonprofit funding intermediaries use performance measurement and why it matters for governance. *Public Performance and Management Review* 33(4): 594–618.

Boris, E., DeLeon, E., Roeger, K., and Nikolova, M. (2010). *Contracts and Grants Between Human Service Nonprofits and Governments*. Washington, DC: Urban Institute, Center on Nonprofits and Philanthropy.

Bratt, R. (2012). The quadruple bottom line and nonprofit housing organizations in the United States. *Housing Studies* 27(4): 438–456.

Bryan, T. (2019). Toward a contingency model for the relationship between capacity and effectiveness in nonprofit organizations. *Nonprofit and Voluntary Sector Quarterly* 48(4): 885–897.

Carman, J. (2009). Nonprofits, funders, and evaluation: Accountability in action. *American Review of Public Administration* 39(4): 374–390

Carman, J., and Fredericks, K. (2010). Evaluation capacity and nonprofit organizations: Is the glass half-empty or half-full? *American Journal of Evaluation* 31(1): 84–104.

Chaney Jones, S. (2014). *Impact & Excellence: Data-driven Strategies for Aligning Mission, Culture, and Performance in Nonprofit and Government Organizations*. Hoboken, NJ: John Wiley & Sons.

Charles, C., and Kim, M. (2016). Do donors care about results? An analysis of nonprofit arts and cultural organizations. *Public Performance and Management Review* 39: 864–884.

Connelly, P., and York, P. (2003). *Building the Capacity of Capacity Builders: A Study of Management Support and Field-Building Organizations in the Nonprofit Sector*. TCC Group. Accessed June 12, 2019. https://www .issuelab.org/resource/building-the-capacity-of-capacity-builders-a -study-of-management-support-and-field-building-organizations-in-the -nonprofit-sector.html.

Coupet, J., and Berrett, J. (2019). Toward a valid approach to nonprofit efficiency measurement. *Nonprofit Management and Leadership* 29: 299–320.

Dart, R. (2004). The legitimacy of social enterprise. *Nonprofit Management and Leadership* 14(4): 411–424.

Dart, R. and Hill, S. (2010). Green matters? An exploration of environmental performance in the nonprofit sector. *Nonprofit Management and Leadership* 20(3): 295–314.

De Lancer Julnes, P., and Holzer, M. (2001). Promoting the utilization of performance measures in public organizations: An empirical study of factors affecting adoption and implementation. *Public Administration Review* 61(6): 693–708.

Gazley, B. (2008). Beyond the contract: The scope and nature of informal government-nonprofit partnerships. *Public Administration Review* 68(1): 141–154.

Gazley, B. (2010). Linking collaborative capacity to performance measurement in government nonprofit partnerships. *Nonprofit and Voluntary Sector Quarterly* 39(4): 653–673.

Gazley, B., and Kissman, K. (2015). *Transformational Governance: How Boards Achieve Extraordinary Change*. Hoboken, NJ: John Wiley & Sons.

Gordon, S. (2001). *Performance-Based Contracting*. Washington, DC: International City/County Management Association.

Gronbjerg, K. (1993). *Understanding Nonprofit Funding: Managing Revenues in Social Services and Community Development Organizations*. Hoboken, NJ: Jossey-Bass.

Gugerty, M., and Karlan, D. (2018). *The Goldilocks Challenge: Right-fit Evidence for the Social Sector*. New York: Oxford University Press.

Illinois Facilities Fund and Donors Forum of Chicago. (1998). *Illinois Nonprofits: Building Capacity for the Next Century*. https://iff.org/wp-content/uploads/2017/05/building_capacity.pdf.

Jeavons, T. (1992). When the management is the message: Relating values to management practice in nonprofit organizations. *Nonprofit Management and Leadership* 2(4): 403–417.

Kaplan, R. (2001). Strategic performance measurement and management in nonprofit organizations. *Nonprofit Management and Leadership* 11(3): 353–370.

Kaplan, R., and Norton, D. (1992). The balanced scorecard: Measures that drive performance. *Harvard Business Review*, January–February 1992.

Keating, E., and Frumkin, P. (2003). Reengineering nonprofit financial accountability: Toward a more reliable foundation for regulation. *Public Administration Review* 63(1): 3–15.

Kim, M., Charles, C., and Pettijohn, S. (2019). Challenges in the use of performance data in management: Results of a national survey of human service organizations. *Public Performance and Management Review* 42(5): 1085–1111.

Knowlton, L., and Phillips, C. (2009). *The Logic Model Guidebook: Better Strategies for Great Results*. Thousand Oaks, CA: Sage.

Kroll, A. (2015). Drivers of performance information use: Systematic literature review and directions for future research. *Public Performance and Management Review* 38: 459–486.

Kushner, R., and Pool, P. (1996). Exploring structure-effectiveness relationships in nonprofit arts organizations. *Nonprofit Management and Leadership* 7(2): 119–136.

Light, P. (2004). *Sustaining Nonprofit Performance*. Washington, DC: Brookings Institution Press.

Martin, L. (2001). *Financial Management for Human Service Administrators*. Boston: Allyn & Bacon.

Martin, L. (2002). Performance-based contracting for human services: Lessons for public procurement? *Journal of Public Performance* 2(1): 55–71.

Martin, L., and Kettner, P. (1996). *Measuring the Performance of Human Service Programs*. Thousand Oaks, CA: Sage.

Metzenbaum, S. (2005). *Performance Accountability: The Five Building Blocks and Six Essential Practices*. Washington, DC: IBM Center for the Business of Government.

Molloy, L. (2010). *Outcome Measurement Strategies Anyone Can Understand*. Iq.

Moore, M. (2003). The public value scorecard: A rejoinder and an alternative to strategic performance measurement and management in non-profit organizations by Robert Kaplan—Working paper #18. Hauser Center for Nonprofit Organizations, Kennedy School of Government, Harvard University, Cambridge, MA.

Morino, M., and Jonas, G. (2001). *Effective Capacity Building in Nonprofit Organizations*. Reston, VA: McKinsey & Company.

Moxham, C. (2010). Help or hindrance? Examining the role of performance measurement in UK nonprofit organizations. *Public Performance and Management Review*. 33(3): 342–354.

Moxham, C., and Boaden, R. (2007). The impact of performance measurement in the voluntary sector: Identification of contextual and processual factors. *International Journal of Operations & Production Management* 27(8): 826–845.

Norman, W., and MacDonald, C. (2004). Getting to the bottom of "triple bottom line." *Business Ethics Quarterly* 14(2): 243–262.

Penna, R. (2011). *The nonprofit Outcomes Toolbox: A Complete Guide to Program Effectiveness, Performance Measurement, and Results*. Hoboken, NJ: John Wiley & Sons.

Prewitt, K. (2006). Foundations. In *The Nonprofit Sector: A Research Handbook*, 2nd ed., edited by Walter W. Powell and Richard Steinberg, 355–375. New Haven, CT: Yale University Press.

Rivenbark, W., and Menter, P. (2006). Building results-based management capacity in nonprofit organizations: The role of local government. *Public Performance and Management Review* 29(3): 255–266.

Rosenzweig, W. (2004). *Double Bottom Line Project Report: Assessing Social Impact in Double Bottom Line Ventures*. UC Berkeley: Center for Responsible Business. https://escholarship.org/uc/item/80n4f1mf.

Salamon, L., ed. (2002). *The Tools of Government: A Guide to the New Governance*. New York: Oxford University Press.

Salamon, L., ed. (2012). *The State of Nonprofit America*. 2nd ed. Washington, DC: Brookings Institution Press.

Schiffer, L. (2021). People, purpose, planet: Adopting a triple bottom line to make the nonprofit arts sector more environmentally sustainable. Master's thesis, Goucher College, Baltimore, MD.

Simon, J. (2001). *The 5 Stages of Nonprofit Organizations.* Saint Paul, MN: Amherst H. Wilder Foundation.

Slatten, L., Guidry, B., and Austin, W. (2011). Accreditation and certification in the non-profit sector: Organizational and economic implications. *Organization Management Journal* 8: 112–127.

Smith, S. (2010). Nonprofits and public administration: Reconciling performance measurement and citizen engagement. *American Review of Public Administration* 40(2): 129–152.

Stephenson, H., Brock, M., and Loughead, M. (2008). Urban Outreach Ministries' organic gardens: Developing a sustainable, triple-bottom-line business for a nonprofit social enterprise. *Journal of the International Academy for Case Studies* 14(8): 69–78.

Thomson, D. (2010). Exploring the role of funders' performance reporting mandates in nonprofit performance measurement. *Nonprofit and Voluntary Sector Quarterly* 39(4): 611–629.

Umar, S., and Hassan, S. (2019). Encouraging the collection of performance data in nonprofit organizations: The importance of organizational support for learning. *Public Performance and Management Review* 42(5): 1062–1084.

US Department of Health and Human Services. (2011). *Managing Data for Performance Improvement.* Health Resources and Services Administration. https://cchn.org/wp-content/uploads/2014/04/managingdataperform anceimprovement.pdf.

Waldron, L., Trusty, B., Nayak, P., and Betancourt, Y. (2020). *What Are Intended Impact and Theory of Change and How Can Nonprofits Use Them?* Boston, MA: The Bridgespan Group. https://www.bridgespan.org /bridgespan/Images/articles/intended-impact-theory-of-change/how -nonprofits-can-use-intended-impact-and-theory-of-change.pdf.

Weisbrod, B. A. (1998). *To Profit or Not to Profit: The Commercial Transformation of the Nonprofit Sector.* Cambridge, UK: Cambridge University Press.

Wyszomirski, M. J. (2013). Shaping a triple-bottom line for nonprofit arts organizations: Micro, macro, and meta policy influences. *Cultural Trends* 22(3–4): 156–166.

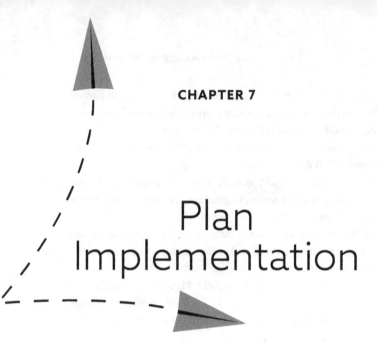

CHAPTER 7

Plan Implementation

KEY POINTS

1. Implementation is just as important as writing the strategic plan itself.
2. To be successful, plan implementation needs to include everyone, from the board and senior staff to frontline staff.
3. To transform plans from a wish list into results takes a dedication of resources, both financial and human.
4. Communicating the plan signals accountability, which is an important part of strengthening internal and external communication.
5. Nonprofits need to treat a strategic plan the same way they treat their financial reports; that is, they should stay up to date on monitoring and regular reporting.

Strategic planning is both a process and a product. Staff and boards need to understand this and dedicate the necessary time and resources to successfully implement a strategic mindset across the organization. Creating the strategic planning document, al-

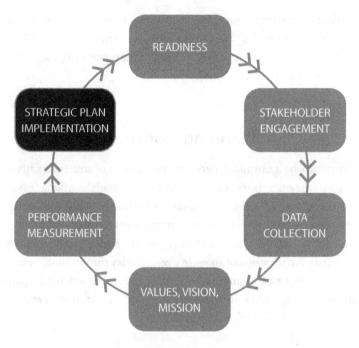

FIGURE 24
Cycle of Strategic Planning

though difficult, is less challenging than actually implementing it. The real work begins when the plan is complete, yet we know little about how nonprofits can and should implement a plan—what works, what doesn't, and what factors affect implementation.

When the demand for a strategic plan comes from outside the organization, the focus is on creating the plan itself, which ignores the challenges of implementation. External pressure for planning can also be perceived as a threat by nonprofit organizations that are reluctant to change and therefore feel vulnerable (Tschirhart et al. 2001). Researchers have explained this as resistance and protective behavior (Feinstein 1985). The process might cause nonprofits to go in a different direction than an organization had intended and, as a result, change its goals (Chandler 1962). This book has outlined the process of strategic planning to help a nonprofit organization create a strategic plan that is responsive to the organization's stakeholders and is grounded in the organization's values, vision, and mission. For plans to be successfully carried out, nonprofits need to be flexible in implementing, monitoring, and evaluating the process (Bryson 2004; Courtney 2002; Koteen 1991).

Planning Horizons

There may be a mismatch between the purpose of strategic plans—to guide the organization over the long term—and the willingness of governing boards to think in the same time frame. Nonprofit boards often have two-year terms, so they might want to focus on a shorter time frame that lines up with their terms. Strategic plans historically covered a broad period of about five years; today shorter time frames, such as three years, are more typical. Of course, in the wake of the pandemic of 2020–2022, it is also perfectly acceptable to look at even shorter time frames of 12–18 months.

Effects of Implementation on Staff

In my years as a consultant, strategic plan implementation has proven to be primarily a staff function, but that's only if the nonprofit has sufficient staff to carry out the plan. Unfortunately, the literature offers little practical guidance (Stone, Bigelow, and Crittenden 1999). When the strategic plan was developed by external experts and consultants, it "represented a significant departure for the organization" (1999). Despite a lack of participation in the process, the staff were still directly responsible for its implementation. Seen through a structural lens, the implementation process reinforced the hierarchical nature of the organization. It also led to redefining roles in the organization and empowered management in decision-making. There was also an opportunity for cultural changes because of participation in the implementation. Strategic plan implementation can result in changes in all four of these dimensions. For broad acceptance and recognition within the organization, it seems that the more effective strategy is to introduce change gradually. Research shows implementation is more challenging when goals are vague or ambiguous and without clear measurements. So, during implementation, goals must be clearly defined and broad terms must be operationalized. This allows for flexibility in plan implementation (Sharp and Brock 2012).

Strategic planning intentionally pulls employees away from their bureaucratic silos toward a broader organizational perspective. This can be challenging and frustrating for lower and mid-level staff because they are absorbed in day-to-day operations. This can also be difficult for senior managers and directors because they must share information across departments, develop broad organizational objectives, provide feedback and guidance to the strategic planning process, and monitor its effectiveness over time.

➤ case example #15

An organization reached out for assistance in implementing a strategic plan that had stalled during the COVID-19 pandemic. At the initial meeting, the consultant met with the executive director and the seven senior program directors. They were seasoned professionals, most had been with the organization for three to five years, and they were running successful programs by all measures. The programs were funded heavily by government, so the directors spent a great deal of time doing compliance reporting. During the pandemic, they had to shift attention to crisis management, and long-term goals fell away. There was little time to think big picture about where the organization was headed and how each program fit with the overall organizational goals. After the first consultation, the consultant and the executive director agreed that the organization wasn't quite ready to tackle implementing the strategic plan. The nonprofit needed to do some internal work first—such as team building and sharing information across the organization—which had suffered during the pandemic.

⅄

Implementation and the Budget

The public administration literature suggests we should develop action plans, and some studies recommend linking strategic priorities to the budget; however, this research comes from the public sector, and it doesn't address how to link strategic plans to the budget within existing bureaucratic structures and organizational cultures (Poister and Streib 2005; Franklin 2000). For nonprofits, there is little to no funding to support strategic planning efforts, and planning can drain the organization in terms of time and resources (see chapter 2). By their very nature, strategic plans deal with "big ideas" that may fall outside the organization's day-to-day activities. While boards are involved at various stages in the creation of a plan, they also need to dedicate resources for implementation through the budgeting process. This is logistically problematic, as nearly all budgets are prepared by departmental function without a separation of funds for strategic planning efforts. More research is needed to determine how strategic planning is implemented and how financial resources are allocated for this purpose.

Now that the strategic plan is ready for implementation, resources must be dedicated to its implementation, and old resources will need to be shifted or new resources attained to support the plan. Both scenarios are possible, but without either, the strategic plan will fail. Also keep in mind that "if the projects and programs selected to be included in a strategic plan are thoroughly implemented, the funds used for those programs are lost opportunities for years to come;" this notion is referred to as "opportunity costs" (Swoboda and Swoboda 2009). The plan itself can be monitored through examination of the budget as well. If the metrics used for certain goals are an increase in resources or a decrease in expenses, then the results of those efforts will show up in the budget reporting documents. The financial statements, whether monthly or quarterly, will be and should be linked to the reporting of the strategic goals since these are tied. A budget is a document that demonstrates the priorities of the organization in dollars. If the strategic goals are priorities, then the budget documents will align with those priorities. Annual budgets should emerge from the goals, objectives, and work plans linked to the organization's strategic plan. "The most difficult task will be justifying the proposed expenditures so they can be tied to the mission goals and objectives and not to emotions or undue non-strategic influences that have no place in a strategic budget" (2009). Sometimes when compromising on goal setting or priorities, goals are massaged so the metrics or outcomes may be vague but budgets are clear. Every organization has finite resources, and the budget makes it very clear where the organization has decided, or not decided, to focus on the goals. The worst outcome is to go through the planning process and not link the budget to the plan. The plan should come first, and the budget should operationalize those goals through dedicated resources. If the strategic plan requires new resources, the budget will outline exactly where those new resources will come from, such as an increase in earned revenue or taking on debt.

Strategic plans may also have goals that impact capital budgets, such as the purchase of new buildings, land, or equipment. The plan needs to be linked to a capital budget to ensure the attainment of those goals. A nonprofit needs to consider all revenue planning strategies against three factors: "mission relevance, financial flexibility, and financial efficiency" (Swoboda and Swoboda 2009). But funding needs to be responsive to the plan rather than the other way around. At the same time, plan implementation may require some financial forecasting, especially if the projects entail significant capital investments. In this case, nonprofits should seek financial experts. The longer the plan duration, the more important it is to consider time as a factor for revenue and expenses.

Reporting the Plan Externally

In the field of public-relations communication, the seminal piece of research most often cited is the *Excellence Study* commissioned by the IABC Research Foundation (Grunig 1992). The research project began with a literature review related to the question of how communication excellence contributes to organizational effectiveness and efficiency. The first book published these literature-review findings (1992). Subsequent books and reports have been products of empirical studies, both qualitative and quantitative, to test the researchers' hypotheses (Dozier, Grunig, and Grunig 1995). According to the authors of the *Excellence Study*, communication is all about relationship building. They identified the seven major public entities affecting most organizations: media, employees, community, customers, members, governments, and investors. For nonprofits, we consider donors to be like investors. The goal of any communications effort is to develop relationships with people. This is best done by identifying a particular audience and focusing the message on their needs and interests. (Grunig and Repper 1992).

Nonprofit administrators who practice effective communication strategies can help stakeholders build social capital (Kruckeberg and Starck 1998). The Chicago School was influential in the development of sociology in the late nineteenth and early twentieth centuries. A group of researchers, including Cooley, Park, and Mead, believed that communication was more than an expression of ideas; it included emotions and attitudes. Even in the face of technology and the information revolution, the basic ideals of the Chicago School of thought can be applied to the community-relations perspective of communication. This perspective embraces the idea of two-way, symmetrical communication and of doing more than persuading and advocating on behalf of organizations; rather, organizations should enter into a dialogue with our communities. Using the Chicago School theoretical framework, researchers identified an approach to community relations based on building a strong sense of community to facilitate communication (1998). We should segment our stakeholders based not on geography but on genuine dialogue, common issues, needs, and so on; this social-interpretive view is called "multicultural community relations" (Banks 1995).

Nonprofit communication, as a specific form of communicating, is far from new. By the mid-1800s, American nonprofit organizations were beginning to experiment with public relations. They sought to gain public support both in terms of their ideas and in raising money for their causes. Early public-relations practitioners in the nonprofit world included the New York Children's Aid Society, the American National Red Cross, the National Education Association, and the Sierra Club (Cutlip 1995). Although there has been a huge increase in the number of nonprofits in the US, the amount of research related to them and, in particular, the management of their communications has not increased proportionately. According to Dozier, Grunig, and Grunig (1995), nonprofit organizations practice only the basic models of public relations—namely, the press-agentry or public-information models—with little two-way, symmetrical communication.

Many reasons might explain why public-relations professionals in nonprofit organizations practice only these basic models, but one reason clearly is the heavy emphasis on fundraising at the expense of public relations. The modern profession of fundraising goes back to the 1920s (Dannelley 1986), when companies specializing in fundraising were formed around the country. These early practitioners used hype, legends, entertainment, and advertising to solicit donations. The worlds of fundraising and public relations collided when fundraisers realized the potential of the media to help in their campaigns. During the 1920s, fundraising and public relations flourished in the post–World War I boom when new public facilities were needed. During the Great Depression and World War II, however, big capital projects ceased. But another boom followed the war, and the cycle of fundraising continued (1986). Today, as a result of decreasing government financial support and the proliferation of charitable organizations, competition for public and private funds is fierce. Nonprofit organizations rely on financial support from a variety of sources to carry out their missions, which means their fundraising departments wield a lot of power. As a result, the matter of public relations is often lost under the fundraising or development banner.

Nonprofit communication relies on the ability to signal to stakeholders that the organization is trustworthy, genuine, effective, and efficient. Accountability is generally defined as the way individuals and organizations are answerable to others and are held responsible for their actions (Bies 2001). Nonprofit participation in voluntary nonprofit standard programs may signal greater accountability to the public and therefore improve trust. Trust and confidence in

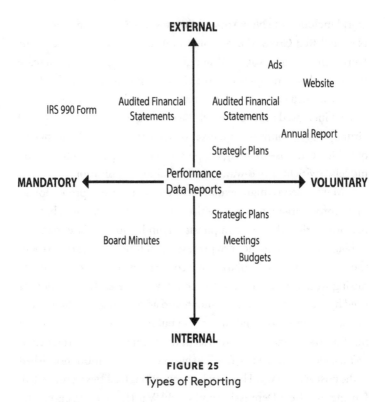

FIGURE 25
Types of Reporting

nonprofit organizations remains high, despite public nonprofit scandals (O'Neill 2009; McDougle, Deitrick, and Donmoyer 2008). Because nonprofit organizations don't have owners and are less regulated than businesses, they have limited reporting responsibilities for their activities (Ostrower and Stone 2006). The figure above suggests reporting can be categorized as internal versus external and voluntary versus mandatory.

In terms of mandatory external reporting, there is only the IRS 990 form, shown in the upper left of the figure. The type of 990 form needed depends on the nonprofit's annual revenues. If the organization exceeds a certain threshold (depending on the state) or receives more than $750,000 from the federal government in a single year, the organization will likely be required to have an independent financial audit, also referred to as a "single audit" (Public Law 104–156, 104th Congress, 1996). As noted, the IRS 990 form is the only document that must be accessible to the public. Performance data reports are at the center of the figure because many factors may determine if these reports are voluntary or mandatory, internal or external. For example, certain funders may require these reports, or they may be for internal purposes only. The right side of the figure refers to all those documents that are voluntary, such as strategic plans. Some of these documents may be made available externally, while others are generally not, such as meeting information and budgets. The IRS and most state laws require nonprofit organizations to keep minutes of their board meetings, so this type of reporting is both internal and mandatory.

Annual reports are voluntary and primarily for external audiences. In fact, annual reports are an excellent tool to share how the implementation of the strategic plan is progressing and to report on key performance metrics. While there is not a lot of research on what annual reports should contain, there is some we can turn to for suggestions. One of the few studies of nonprofit performance reporting found annual reports for museums were highly variable in content and size. The results did not vary by independent variables such as museum ownership, type, organizational age, or accreditation. The annual reports in this study were analyzed by assigning each page to one of nine categories: cover and table of contents, letters, programs and collections, museum personnel, fundraising activities, donor recognition, attendance data, numeric or graphic data, and financial data. The pages were used as an indication of museum management's focus. Nearly one-third of the reports did not contain any information about expenses for administration or fundraising. These findings indicate the variability of annual reports, even for a group of nonprofit organizations with similar missions (Christenson and Mohr 2003). Other researchers identified best practices on five dimensions of financial and nonfinancial information: completeness, accessibility, transparency, full disclosure, and relevance. They studied a sample of 105 nonprofit organizations in four different categories: environmental, disease research, poverty, and emergency relief. They recommended that complete audited financial statements should be part of the annual reports and that the annual reports should be available online for at least five years (Gordon et al. 2010). Additionally, annual reports should include quantitative and qualitative information for a richer and more complete story of the organization's goals and successes (Greatbanks and Elkin 2010).

If an organization has gone through the cycle of strategic planning, then it should also communicate the plan to all its stakeholders. Having a current strategic plan is a signal the organization is committed to its own long-term sustainability. While not legally required, sharing the document and communicating about its implementation speaks to organizational transparency and supports voluntary accountability. Researchers found that while internal voluntary accountability does not affect the public's attitude toward a nonprofit, lower levels of accountability are associated with lower levels of public trust, reputation, perceived quality, and donation behavior (Becker 2018, 562).

One way to improve reporting is to produce these voluntary reports, including a strategic plan, and make them available online. Online accountability (also known as "web-based accountability" or "virtual accountability") is one aspect of the larger concept of accountability and emerged in the early 2000s. Saxton and Guo (2011) found the most significant factors supporting higher online accountability were asset size and board performance. Other researchers have determined that improved online accountability is related to the interactivity and multimedia orientation of an organization's website (Jo and Kim 2003). Some researchers have described web-based accountability as having two dimensions—disclosure and dialogue—and have found that nonprofits are better at disclosing information than creating dialogue for true civic engagement (Saxton and Guo 2011). Researchers noted that organizations making better use of online disclosure tools in areas of performance and finances fared better and raised more money (Saxton, Neely, and Guo 2014). More recently, research has shown that smaller and younger organizations are better at online accountability efforts than those that are larger and older. In addition, smaller organizations are more flexible and exist in an organizational climate that facilitates quicker adoption and implementation of online accountability practices (Lee, Pendharkar, and Blouin 2012). Other scholars contend that organizations that don't implement elements of online accountability related to their finances and performance may not be able to survive in the current environment of openness and transparency (Lee and Joseph 2012).

Monitoring and Reporting Internally

Any strategic plan needs to be monitored to be carried out successfully. As discussed earlier, the strategic plan needs to be tied to annual work plans for staff and annual goals for the board. These work plans and goals should be monitored with regular frequency. I recommend that the board examine the progress toward goals as often and as much as it monitors its financial condition, whether that's monthly or quarterly at scheduled board meetings. To make this task less burdensome, staff should prepare a progress report in a simple document using a template such as the following.

Several resources are available to help organizations create visuals to depict their plan progress. Since the 1980s, dashboards have been used to illustrate this kind of information. In the 1990s, the Balanced Scorecard approach allowed companies to identify key performance indicators (KPIs) that could then be displayed on a dashboard (Kaplan and Norton 1992). Dashboards are data-driven, allowing users to visualize any type of data, from sales and memberships

1.				
Date Revised:				
Target Completion Date:	Status: ☐ On Schedule ☐ Behind Schedule ☐ Complete		Budget:	Point Person:
Progress:				Activity Team:
Notes:				

FIGURE 26
Strategic Goal—Action Plan Worksheet

to donations, program participation, and more. The key is to figure out what the metrics will be for each of your strategic goals; deciding whether visualizing those metrics will be beneficial for internal purposes, the staff, and the board; and determining how flexible the reporting is. For example, maybe the board will want to examine this information at the department level, but staff may want to monitor data at the program level. Both choices should be possible and planned for.

Boards and staff should also consider whether they want to make this form of data visualization accessible outside the organization and which metrics would be appropriate for that. For example, an organization may wish to report externally on the overall progress toward the strategic goals but not on specific objectives within each program. Many decisions need to be made before data visualization is considered. These include the type of data collected and metrics used for each strategic goal, the validity of the data collected, and the systems needed to input and analyze that data at the correct level (individual, program, department, or organization) (Healy 2019; Evergreen 2014; Smiciklas 2012; Yau 2011; Few 2006). Several fundraising platforms also offer some kind of data visualization. For example, Salesforce and its training program called Salesforce Nonprofit Cloud are available online at no cost. Salesforce offers 10 subscriptions to the Nonprofit Success Pack for free as part of its Power of Us Program. Eligible nonprofits must be 501(c)(3) organizations (Salesforce n.d.). Anyone can learn how to use Salesforce for free through their training platform called Trailhead (Trailhead n.d.).

Most sales and fundraising software platforms have data analysis or visualization capabilities; alternatively, your data can be easily exported into a program such as Tableau. Tableau offers free licenses for small nonprofits defined as having an annual budget under $5 million. Tableau also has a volunteer service corps to help nonprofits use the platform (Tableau n.d.). Another option is Alteryx, a program that can manipulate large data sets for analysis (Alteryx n.d.) The company offers platform licenses for free or at a reduced cost to small nonprofits. For a free license, nonprofits must have an annual income of less than $10 million (n.d.). Alteryx also created Alteryx for Good

Co-Lab, which is a group of volunteers who provide analytic expertise to nonprofit organizations at no cost (Alteryx Gives Back n.d.). Regardless of how the nonprofit organization reports goal progress (in a simple spreadsheet or document, or by using a dashboard), monitoring is critical to ensure successful implementation of the strategic plan.

The Planning Cycle Begins Anew

In this book, I've outlined how a nonprofit organization of any size can embark on a strategic planning process that's easy to follow. In particular, I wrote the book for the majority of nonprofits in the US with limited resources and small staffs. I've also explained here how strategic planning is a cyclical process, and sometimes you may have to go back a step because of a disruption, like the pandemic and its aftermath. As we've seen, an organization always needs to think about the road ahead, even if where it will lead isn't quite predictable. And when a strategic plan runs out of data, because of either circumstances or time, it's time to begin anew. This book is meant for nonprofit leaders who want to understand not only the latest research but also the practical aspects of working through a strategic planning process. I hope the book has outlined a process that is neither intimidating nor expensive. It is a thoughtful process, ideally inclusive of all stakeholders, based on the right data, and given the attention it deserves throughout implementation. No one wants to waste resources on plans that are too vague, based on bad data, or poorly implemented. Instead, strategic plans should energize and motivate individuals to work toward a shared vision. That leads to a truly successful plan.

DISCUSSION QUESTIONS

1. How can strategic goals be turned into annual work plans and objectives for staff?
2. Why and how should a strategic plan be tied to an organization's budget?

3. How should nonprofit organizations think about voluntary disclosure to inspire trust and loyalty from their stakeholders?
4. What are some ways organizations can monitor their progress toward goal completion?

REFERENCES

Alteryx. (n.d.). Accessed February 20, 2022. https://www.alteryx.com/.

Alteryx Gives Back. (n.d.). Accessed February 20, 2022. https://www.afgcolab.com/.

Banks, S. (1995). *Multicultural Public Relations: A Social-Interpretive Approach.* Thousand Oaks, CA: Sage.

Becker, A. (2018). An experimental study of voluntary nonprofit accountability and effects on public trust, reputation, perceived quality, and donation behavior. *Nonprofit and Voluntary Sector Quarterly* 47(3): 562–582.

Bies, A. (2001). Accountability, organizational capacity and continuous improvement: Findings from Minnesota's nonprofit sector. *New Directions for Philanthropic Fundraising* 4(31): 51–80.

Bryson, J. (2004). *Strategic Planning for Public and Nonprofit Organizations: A Guide to Strengthening and Sustaining Organizational Achievement.* 3rd ed. Hoboken, NJ: Jossey-Bass.

Chandler, A. (1962). *Strategy and Structure.* Cambridge, MA: MIT Press.

Christenson, A., and Mohr, R. (2003). Not-for-profit annual reports: What do museum managers communicate? *Financial Accountability and Management* 19(2): 139–158.

Courtney, R. (2002). *Strategic Management for Voluntary Nonprofit Organizations.* New York: Routledge.

Cutlip, S. (1995). *Public Relations History: From the 17th to the 20th Century.* Mahwah, NJ: Lawrence Erlbaum.

Dannelley, P. (1986). *Fundraising and Public Relations.* Norman, OK: University of Oklahoma Press.

Dozier, D., Grunig, G., and Grunig, L. (1995). *Manager's Guide to Excellence in Public Relations and Communications Management.* Mahwah, NJ: Lawrence Erlbaum.

Evergreen, S. (2014). *Presenting Data Effectively: Communicating Your Findings for Maximum Impact.* Thousand Oaks, CA: Sage.

Feinstein, K. (1985). Innovative management in turbulent times: Large-scale agency change. *Administration in Social Work* 9: 35–46.

Few, S. (2006). *Information Dashboard Design: The Effective Visual Communication of Data*. Sebastopol, CA: O'Reilly Media Inc.

Franklin, A. (2000). An examination of bureaucratic reactions to institutional controls. *Public Performance and Management Review* 24(1): 8–21.

Gordon, T., Khumawala, S., Kraut, M., and Neely, D. (2010). Five dimensions of effectiveness for nonprofit annual reports. *Nonprofit Management and Leadership* 21(2): 209–228.

Greatbanks, R., and Elkin, G. (2010). The use and efficacy of anecdotal performance reporting in the third sector. *International Journal of Productivity* 59(6): 571–585.

Grunig, J. (1992). Symmetrical systems of internal communication. In *Excellence in Public Relations and Communication Management*, edited by James E. Grunig, 531–576. Mahwah, NJ: Lawrence Erlbaum.

Grunig, J., and Repper, F. (1992). Strategic management, publics and issues. In *Excellence in Public Relations and Communications Management*, edited by James E. Grunig, 117–157. Mahwah, NJ: Lawrence Erlbaum.

Healy, K. (2019). *Data Visualization: A Practical Introduction*. Princeton, NJ: Princeton University Press.

Jo, S., and Kim, Y. (2003). The effect of web characteristics on relationship building. *Journal of Public Relations Research* 15(3): 199–223.

Kaplan, R., and Norton, D. (1992). The balanced scorecard—Measures that drive performance. *Harvard Business Review*, January–February 1992.

Koteen, J. (1991). *Strategic Management in Public and Nonprofit Organizations*. Westport, CT: Praeger.

Kruckeberg, D., and Starck, K. (1998). *Public Relations and Community: A Reconstructed Theory*. Westport, CT: Praeger.

Lee, R., and Joseph, R. (2012). Survival of the fittest: Online accountability in complex organizational populations. Proceedings of the Southern Association for Information Systems Conference, Atlanta, GA, March 23–24, 2012.

Lee, R., Pendharkar, P., and Blouin, M. (2012). An exploratory examination of the implementation of online accountability: A technological innovation perspective. *Journal of Information Technology Management* 23(3): 1–11.

McDougle, L., Deitrick, L., and Donmoyer, R. (2008). *The Appreciated Sector: Public Confidence in San Diego County Nonprofit Organizations*. San Diego: Caser Family Center for Nonprofit Research, University of San Diego.

O'Neill, M. (2009). Public confidence in public charitable nonprofits. *Nonprofit and Voluntary Sector Quarterly* 38(2): 237–269.

Ortmann, A., and Schlesinger, M. (2003). Trust, repute and the role of nonprofit enterprise. In *The Study of Nonprofit Enterprise: Theories and*

Approaches, edited by H. Anheier and A. Ben-Nur, 77–114. New York: Springer.

Ostrower, F., and Stone, M. (2006). Governance: Research trends, gaps, and future prospects. In *The Nonprofit Sector: A Research Handbook*, edited by Richard Steinberg and Walter Powell, 612–628. New Haven, CT: Yale University Press.

Poister, T., and Streib, G. (2005). Elements of strategic planning and management in municipal government: Status after two decades. *Public Administration Review* 65(1): 45–56.

Public Law 104–156, 104th Congress. (1996). *Single Audit Act Amendments*. https://obamawhitehouse.archives.gov/sites/default/files/omb/assets/about_omb/104-156.pdf.

Salesforce. (n.d.). Power of Us. Accessed February 20, 2022. https://www.salesforce.org/power-of-us/.

Saxton, G., and Guo, C. (2011). Accountability online: Understanding the web-based accountability practices of nonprofit organizations. *Nonprofit and Voluntary Sector Quarterly* 40(2): 270–295.

Saxton, G., Neely, D., and Guo, C. (2014). Web disclosure and the market for charitable contributions. *Journal of Accounting and Public Policy* 33(2): 127–144.

Sharp, Z., and Brock, D. (2012) Implementation through risk mitigation: Strategic processes in the nonprofit organization. *Administration and Society* 44(5): 571–594.

Smiciklas, M. (2012). *The Power of Infographics: Using Pictures to Communicate and Connect with Your Audiences*. New York: Pearson Education.

Steinberg, R., and Gray, B. (1993). The role of nonprofit enterprise in 1993: Hansmann revisited. *Nonprofit and Voluntary Sector Quarterly* 22(4): 297–316.

Stone, M., Bigelow, B., and Crittenden, W. (1999). Research on strategic management in nonprofit organizations: Synthesis, analysis and future directions. *Administration and Society* 31: 378–423.

Swoboda, D., and Swoboda, G. (2009). *Managing Nonprofit Financial and Fiscal Operations*. Tysons Corners, VA: Management Concepts.

Tableau. (n.d.). Accessed February 20, 2022. https://www.tableau.com/.

Tschirhart, M., Mesch, D., Perry, J., Miller, T., and Lee, G. (2001). Stipended volunteers: Their goals, experiences, satisfaction, and likelihood of future service. *Nonprofit and Voluntary Sector Quarterly* 30: 422–443.

Trailhead. (n.d.). Trailhead for Salesforce. Accessed February 20, 2022. https://trailhead.salesforce.com/.

Yau, N. (2011). *Visualize This: The Flowing Data Guide to Design, Visualization, and Statistics*. Hoboken, NJ: Wiley Publishing Inc.

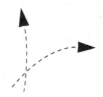

Strategic Planning Readiness Assessment

The readiness or capacity of an organization to engage successfully in a deliberative, reasonably disciplined strategic planning process should be clearly understood by the organization's leadership, and perhaps other key stakeholders, before a formal planning process is begun.

TABLE 7. PLANNING READINESS CHECKLIST

1. We have a clear understanding of our formal mission.	YES	NO
2. We have an inspiring mission.	YES	NO
3. We know who our key and other stakeholders are, and how they relate to one another and to us.	YES	NO
4. We have a clear understanding of our organization's strengths, weaknesses, opportunities, and challenges (or threats).	YES	NO
5. We understand our organization's culture and values.	YES	NO
6. There are board champions of our strategic planning effort.	YES	NO
7. There are capable staff to manage the strategic planning process and efforts.	YES	NO
8. There is an effective team of board members and staff to lead the planning effort.	YES	NO

(Continued)

Adapted from Worksheet 6, in John M. Bryson and Farnum K. Alston, *Creating Your Strategic Plan: A Workbook for Public and Nonprofit Organizations*, 3rd ed. (San Francisco: Jossey-Bass, 2011).

TABLE 7. (CONTINUED)

9. The team can access appropriate and necessary analyses and resources to support the process.	YES NO
10. The team has or can develop processes to include (as appropriate) both internal and external stakeholders.	YES NO
11. We have effective groups already in place to promote deliberation, learning, and informed decision-making as part of the strategic planning process.	YES NO
12. We consistently learn in formal and informal ways from our successes and challenges.	YES NO
13. We have or will be able to develop adequate funding for our anticipated key strategies.	YES NO
14. We have or can develop an effective communications plan for the strategic planning process.	YES NO
15. We can plan for short-term wins that demonstrate progress and action and can lead to long-term gains.	YES NO
16. We can anticipate resistance to change and work to address it.	YES NO
17. We can adapt the organization's leadership development agenda to the strategic plan.	YES NO
18. We can develop incentives and human-resource plans (paid staff and volunteers) and procedures around the strategic plan.	YES NO
19. We can develop our budgets and resource expenditures around the strategic plan.	YES NO
20. We can develop our information-technology budgets and processes around the strategic plan.	YES NO

Given the responses to these statements, we should choose from the following next steps:

- Proceed with strategic planning
- Figure out whether and how to change any "No" answers to "Yes"
- Postpone strategic planning for now

Sample Request for Proposal

St. Charles Public Library
One South Sixth Avenue
St. Charles IL 60174-2195
630-584-0076, Fax 630-584-9262
www.scpld.org

REQUEST FOR PROPOSAL (RFP)
STRATEGIC PLANNING PROCESS & FACILITATION
ST. CHARLES PUBLIC LIBRARY DISTRICT
APRIL 2017

Submittal Due Date and Time: Thursday, May 4, 2017, by 5:00 p.m. CST
Interviews Conducted: Week of May 8–12, 2017
Submittal shall be submitted to:
St. Charles Public Library District
One South Sixth Avenue
St. Charles, IL 60174-2195
Attn: Edith G. Craig, Library Director
Number of Copies: Submit 1 electronic and 7 hard copies of the proposal
Submittals submitted by fax or email will not be accepted.
Offers may not be withdrawn for a period of 90 days after proposal due date without the consent of the St. Charles Public Library District.

The St. Charles Public Library District reserves the right to reject any and all submittals or parts thereof, to waive any irregularities or informalities in proposal procedures, and to award the contract in a manner best serving the interest of the Library. The Library will not return any materials received in response to this invitation.

Submittals will not be opened in a public forum.

I. Statement of Purpose

The St. Charles Public Library District (Library) has prepared this Request for Proposal in order to retain the services of a qualified firm to assist in the facilitation of a comprehensive strategic planning process and analyze the information to produce a 3–5 year strategic planning document.

The Library would like to incorporate various tools to make sure all Library stakeholders are considered when creating the guiding document. The document should be reflective of all of the feedback obtained during all engagement sessions with the various stakeholders.

II. Background

For over 125 years, the St. Charles community has supported and benefited from a library. The Library is governed by an elected seven-member Board of Trustees. The Board provides policy direction over the Library system. They are responsible for final approval of the Library's Budget and Tax Levy. Current services are financed through property tax revenue, fees, fines, public donations, and State and Federal aid. The Library provides a general collection of books, magazines, periodicals, electronic resources, and multi-media materials. The Library is part of a consortium that provides an online public catalog that has location and availability information among all of the libraries. The Library maintains a website (www.scpld.org) that serves a variety of information and service needs 24 hours a day, including access to a range of licensed databases and e-books, music, and other downloadable material.

The Library serves a population slightly over 55,000 and circulates over 1.5 million items. There are approximately 30,500 cardholders in our Library, which means there is a portion of our population that is not served by the Library. In addition to these two groups of people, the Library has a Foundation and a Friends group that contribute immensely to the success of the Library. There are donors and volunteers to consider when obtaining feedback as well, which will help the Library serve in its mission. And last but not least, the Board of Trustees and staff play an integral part of the operations and success of the Library.

While the Library District serves all of the St. Charles city limits, there are other villages that the district incorporates. Attached is the City Community Profile for reference (appendix A). The District also includes parts of South Elgin, Wayne, and West Chicago.

The Library currently has a Strategic Plan that will end in 2017 (appendix B).

III. Project Objective

The Library seeks assistance to help develop a guiding document to establish the long-term (3–5 years) future of the direction of the SCPL by:

  a) Reaching our stakeholders (not in any particular order):
      i) Patrons
      ii) Community-at-large (people who live in the district and not current SCPL patrons)
      iii) Board
      iv) Staff
      v) Volunteers
      vi) Friends of the SCPL
      vii) SCPL Foundation
      viii) Donors
  b) Using tools that can include (but are not limited to):
      i) Surveys (print, online, available in Spanish)
      ii) Focus groups
      iii) Community input sessions in various locations with various groups or organizations
      iv) One-on-one meetings with key stakeholders
      v) Other methods identified by the successful firm

IV. Scope of Work

The process will incorporate all of these stakeholders using a variety of tools. An analysis of the information and feedback should be incorporated when drafting the final strategic planning document.

The Library seeks to answer the following questions as part of the study:

  a) If people don't use our Library's services—why?
  b) What does the community feel is lacking in our community and how can we help fill those gaps within our mission?

c) Does the community feel that the SCPL should renovate or expand the Library? Why or why not?

d) How do our current patrons feel about the Library? And how can we improve?

e) What do our residents feel is lacking in our community? How can the Library fit those needs? Does meeting those needs fall within our mission?

The Library would like to advocate for the need to renovate or expand our building when using these tools. We'd like to offer (not a comprehensive list):

a) Tours of the Library (public spaces and back-office spaces)

b) Literature and materials that attest to our needs for more programming, meeting rooms, and collaborative spaces

c) Chances for the community to talk about the Library with the Director and Board members during these input sessions, focus groups, etc.

d) A chance to promote services to the community while engaging in these events

V. Library Resources

The Library will provide any in-house information that the successful consultant may require to facilitate, analyze, and produce a plan in a timely manner. The Library will assist in marketing any community sessions or other tools used by the successful firm. The Library will help make the contact for the different groups so that the process happens smoothly.

VI. Basic Tasks and Deliverables

We would like an experienced, professional firm to help us perform, at a minimum, the following:

a) Facilitate one or more sessions with staff and board members to identify the Library's core values.

b) Facilitate a session with the Library Board (and perhaps members of the staff management team) to identify the Library's purpose. (This may involve the development of a new mission statement.)

c) Facilitate the planning process. Work with the Board and staff to gather data through research (various tools aforementioned) and community input to identify how the Library's values and purpose can be aligned with current priorities and needs of the community to form the basis of the Library's strategic focus for the next 3–5 years.

d) Develop a strategic plan document, based on the results of the planning process, that will be communicated to the Library's stakeholders. The final deliverable should include specification of the Library's purpose, values, and core services as well as clearly defined areas of strategic focus.

e) Submit a draft strategic plan to the Director for review, and modify it as needed.

f) Prepare and submit a final version of the strategic plan to the Director. Provide a written and electronic manual and final plan document.

g) All raw and summary data is to be delivered to the Library at the conclusion of the planning process.

h) Additional activities may be suggested by bidders. Potentially, following the award of a contract, additional services may be identified by the Library or consultant. In order to facilitate the possibility of additional services, the consultant is requested to provide a listing of the hourly billable rates for those persons assigned to this contract. No amendment may be entered into without prior authorization by the Library.

VII. Schedule

Below is the estimated timeline for the search for the consulting firm. The following schedule is subject to change. Except as provided below, changes will only be made by written amendment to this RFP.

TABLE 8. EXAMPLE OF RFP TIMELINE

Estimated date	Event
April 24, 2017	Release Request for Proposals
May 4, 2017	Proposals due
May 8–May 12, 2017	Interviews conducted
By June 14, 2017	Library Board awards contract (subject to delay without notice to proposers)

VIII. Questions

Proposers will be required to submit any questions in writing before the close of business Monday, May 1, 2017, in order for staff to prepare written responses. Questions are best received and most quickly responded to when sent via email directly to ecraig@stcharleslibrary.org. Questions will not be accepted by phone.

IX. Corrections and Addenda

a) If a proposer discovers any ambiguity, conflict, discrepancy, omission, or other error in this RFP, the proposer shall immediately notify the contact person of such error in writing and request clarification or modification of the document. Modifications will be made by addenda as indicated below to all parties in receipt of this RFP.

b) If a proposer fails to notify the contact person prior to the date fixed for submission of proposals of a known error in the RFP, or an error that reasonably should have been known, the proposers shall submit a proposal at their risk, and if the proposer is awarded a contract they shall not be entitled to additional compensation or time by reason of the error or its subsequent correction.

c) Addenda issued by the Library interpreting or changing any of the items in this RFP, including all modifications thereof, shall be incorporated in the proposal. The proposers shall submit the addenda cover sheet with the proposal (or deliver them to the Library Director's Office, St. Charles Public Library, One South Sixth Street, St. Charles, IL 60174-2195, if the proposer has previously submitted a proposal to the Library). Any oral communication by the Library's designated contact person or any other Library staff member concerning this RFP is not binding on the Library and shall in no way modify this RFP or any obligations arising hereunder.

X. Proposal Format and Contents

For ease of review and to facilitate evaluation, the proposals for this project should be organized and presented in the order requested as follows:

a) Section One: Organizational Information: Provide specific information concerning the firm in this section, including the

SAMPLE REQUEST FOR PROPOSAL 🌣 175

legal name, address, and telephone number of your company. Include the name and telephone number of the person(s) in your company authorized to execute the proposed contract. Provide a description of the firm, number of years in business, and its core competencies. Identify the key personnel and their backups who will be assigned to the program.

b) Section Two: Qualifications and Experience: Provide specific information in this section concerning the firm's experience in the services specified in this RFP. Provide specific information on projects that have included the facilitation of strategic planning for public libraries. Examples of projects, as current as possible, should be submitted. References are required. Please provide names, addresses, and telephone numbers of contact persons with three client agencies for whom similar services have been provided.

c) Section Three: Project Approach and Work Schedule: Provide a description of the methodology developed to perform all required services, with an aggressive schedule that will complete within 6–7 months, if possible. This projected schedule should contain specific milestones and dates of completion which will be used to set schedules. Also identify the extent of Library personnel involvement deemed necessary, including key decision points at each stage of the project. Information as to the type of any software that is anticipated to be used in the planning process should also be mentioned.

d) Section Four: Cost of Service: The proposal shall clearly state ALL of the costs associated with the project, broken down by category of products and services, and all ongoing costs for recommended or required products and services, such as maintenance. The project costs must be broken out and include all expenses that will be charged to the Library, including but not limited to hourly rates for labor, software costs, software maintenance costs, implementation fees, shipping, insurance, communications, documentation reproduction, and all expenses, including travel, meal reimbursement, hotel per diems, taxes, etc. Failure to clearly identify all costs associated with the proposal may be cause for rejection of the consultant's proposal.

176 Å APPENDIX B

e) <u>Section Five: Identification of Subcontractors:</u> Proposers shall identify all subcontractors they intend to use for the proposed scope of work. For each subcontractor listed, proposers shall indicate: 1. What products and/or services are to be supplied by that subcontractor, and 2. What percentage of the overall scope of work that subcontractor will perform.

f) <u>Section Six: Additional Information:</u> Include any other information you believe to be pertinent but not required.

XI. Selection Process

a) Selection criteria refers to the qualifications that the Library would require in order to award a contract for services, or qualifications that the Library intends on using to evaluate proposals in order to select the most qualified proposal for the project. At a minimum, respondents must provide all the requested information in this RFP. The Library will consider:

   i) Demonstrated ability to perform services described
   ii) Experience, qualifications, and expertise
   iii) Quality of work as verified by references
   iv) Costs relative to the scope of services
   v) A demonstrated history of providing similar services to comparable entities
   vi) The locality of the proposer

b) The Library may, during the evaluation process, request from any proposer additional information which the Library deems necessary to determine the proposer's ability to perform the required services. If such information is requested, the proposer shall be permitted two business days to submit the information requested.

c) The Library reserves the right to select the proposal which, in its sole judgement, best meets the needs of the Library.

d) All firms responding to this RFP will be notified of their selection or non-selection after the Library has completed the selection process.

e) Generally, the firm selected by the Library will be recommended to the Library Board for this project, but the Library Board is not bound to accept the recommendation or award the project to the recommended firm.

f) After initial screening, the Library may select those firms deemed most qualified for this project for further evaluation. Interviews of these selected firms will be conducted as part of the final selection process. Interviews may have their own separate scoring during the evaluation process.

XII. General Information

a) Rules and Regulations: The issuance of this solicitation does not constitute an award commitment on the part of the Library, and the Library shall not pay for costs incurred in the preparation or submission of proposals. All costs and expenses associated with the preparation of this proposal shall be borne by the proposer.

b) The Library reserves the right to reject any or all proposals or portions thereof if the Library determines that it is in the best interest of the Library to do so.

c) All proposers submit their proposals to the Library with the understanding that the recommended selection of the Library is final and subject only to review and final approval by the Library Director and the Library Board. Upon submission, all proposals shall be treated as confidential documents until the selection process is completed.

d) Nonliability of Library: The Library shall not be liable for any precontractual expenses incurred by the proposer or selected contractor(s). The Library shall be held harmless and free from any and all liability, claims, or expenses whatsoever incurred by, or on behalf of, any person or organization responding to this RFP.

e) Proposal Alternatives: Proposers may not take exception or make material alterations to any requirement of the RFP. Alternatives to the RFP may be submitted as separate proposals and so noted on the cover of the proposal. The Library reserves the right to consider such alternative proposals, and to award an agreement based thereon if it is determined to be in the Library's best interest and such proposal satisfies all minimum qualifications specified in the RFP. Please indicate clearly in the proposal that the proposal offers an alternative to the RFP.

f) Form of Agreement: No agreement with the Library shall have any effect until a contract has been signed by both parties.

g) Withdrawal and Submission of Modified Proposal: A proposer may withdraw a proposal at any time prior to the submission deadline by submitting a written notification of withdrawal signed by the proposer or his/her authorized agent. Another proposal may be submitted prior to the deadline. A proposal may not be changed after the deadline for submission.

INDEX

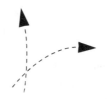